Conversations with
Andrew Greeley

Conversations with
Andrew Greeley

Ronald D. Pasquariello

Quinlan Press
Boston

Published by Quinlan Press
131 Beverly Street, Boston, MA 02114

Printed in the United States of America, 1988.

Library of Congress Cataloging-in-Publication Data

Greeley, Andrew M., 1928-
  Conversations with Andrew Greeley.

  1. Greeley, Andrew M., 1928-   —Interviews.
2. Novelists, American—20th century—Interviews.
3. Catholic Church—United States—Clergy—Interviews.
I. Pasquariello, Ronald D.   II. Title.
PS3557.R358Z465   1988   813'.54   88-42812
ISBN 1-55770-068-0

To my friend, Paul R. Caruso, a wonderful example of sacramental imagination.

This book grows out of a friendship with a remarkable person. I am deeply grateful to Andrew Greeley for his time, his interest, his encouragement and his sense of humor.

I must also acknowledge many others whose assistance was so cheerfully given. Among them: June Rosner and Marilyn Liss of Rosner & Liss Public Relations; Mary Kotecki of the National Opinion Research Center; and Alice Rubio of Andrew Greeley Enterprises. All of these worthy persons made the production of this book a pleasure. May every author experience such gracious cooperation in the tedious task of bringing a manuscript to publication.

The portrait of Andrew Greeley on the jacket of this book is the work of Chicago sculptor and artist John David Mooney.

CONTENTS

Introduction

One of the most fascinating weeks in my life was the week I spent in conversation with Andrew Greeley. I've known the man as a friend for over a decade. We've been associated with each other on a few projects, but I'd never sat down to discuss his ideas on so many topics in such depth.

I have not been successful in finding a single metaphor to describe his productivity. What can you say about a man who has published three novels and two scholarly works in the past year? I remember an episode of "Star Trek" in which the crew of the Enterprise stood by wide-eyed as an invisible Dr. Spock buzzed around the starship. In quick succession, one mechanical problem after another was repaired. Similarly, Andrew Greeley seems to operate in a different time frame than most of us—an hour on our biological clocks is about a minute on his. Whatever the satisfactory metaphor, he writes faster than I can read!

Hegel said a great man is plagued by one thought. One of the things that impresses me about Andrew Greeley is his remarkable consistency. Everything he does is shaped by a single vision, the Catholic social ethic which makes person, place and pluralism central, and which has a profound respect for microstructures like neighborhoods and communities. He explores that ethic in his nonfiction and exalts it in his fiction.

Greeley's candor is disarming. He has been so very often misunderstood, yet he answered every question I asked him, and he answered each with complete confidence that I would not distort his intention or meaning. His faith is passionate. God is his lover. You can see that in his eyes when conversation takes a turn to things religious. His joy in his priesthood is comforting—finding someone so happy in his profession is becoming more and more difficult.

Greeley's friends and readers are very fortunate indeed, because his loyalty to them is fierce. Thousands of his readers write to him about the love of church, God or religion that his novels have inspired in them. In return, every word that pops up on the screen of his word processor is shaped by his fidelity to the concerns of his readers.

He has a sharp tongue, but he uses it for seasoning. He's passionate about life—his, yours, the church's, God's. If you don't like your Andrew Greeley plain, then he'll serve it up with some spice. And that's just one more thing that made conversations with him so enjoyable.

I
WRITING

''God does intend happy endings.''

Francesco Scavullo

If Jesus were alive today, would he be sitting in Nazareth writing novels?

That's not a good question because it tries to project back into that culture a situation which could not be envisaged in his culture. Jesus was a storyteller. The kinds of stories that get to people today most effectively are novels and screenplays. So, I would say much more modestly that writing novels is certainly consistent with what Jesus did.

Is that why you write stories?

Basically, yes. They're a priestly work.

In what sense are they a priestly work?

They're stories of God's love. The same as the parables of Jesus. They don't have the literary quality of the parables of Jesus, nothing does, but they have the same content.

And the priestly work is to do what with God's love?

It's supposed to reveal it, to disclose it; to assure people once again that that's what their faith is about—God's forgiving love, and the opportunity to begin again. Second chances, if you will. If there's one overarching theme in all my novels, it's that people get second chances. And third, fourth, fifth and twentieth chances.

Are all your novels comedies?

Comedy, of course, is a word that can be used in many different senses. They are certainly comedies in the classic sense of that word in that they have hopeful endings. I am not capable of writing a story that has a tragic ending, though I don't deny the validity of tragedy as a literary form.

They're also comic—and they tend to be increasingly comic—in that they are funny. There are very funny people in them. Some of these funny people say very funny things. they get more and more comic as time goes on.

When you apply the word "comic" to God, do you mean the same thing?

Yes. First of all, God does intend happy endings. To quote Juliana of Norwich—on something that, since I saw you last, has been written

3

into the story I'm working on—"All manner of things will be well."
So, God is comic in this sense.

But I also think God is comic in that She is vastly amused by us,
as most parents are by funny little children.

And is God the real hero of your novels?

Oh, yes. Yes, yes. God is the real hero—God and the Holy Spirit,
of course, which is God, dancing whither She will, and drawing all
things to Her own purposes.

Do you write to edify?

Oh, no, no, no, no. That would be terrible to do. Stories that are
written to uplift or to edify are perversions of stories. That's what some
of the critics on the Left as well as the Right want from me.

James Finn, in a review of one of my books in the *Wall Street
Journal*—it was a nice review—said that "Father Greeley writes novels
so that, by entertaining, he educates." I understand what he means,
but I don't think that's an accurate description. Again, that's misus-
ing story, it's perverting it.

How do you expect your readers to react to your novels?

Hopefully, they will close the book at the end, realizing that it is
always springtime in human life, that one can always begin again. Even
if beginning again is going to cause horrendous conflict and trouble,
it's always possible to begin again.

If you want to say that communicating that possibility to people
is a form of edification, okay, fine. But that's not how most of the folks
who want edifying stories define "edify."

And who are the people that read your novels?

There's lots of them—though, of course, there's never enough! About
60 to 65 percent of them are women. About the same proportion of
them are Catholic. They tend to be high school- and heavily college-
educated; between twenty and forty-five. About half of them don't
go to church regularly. They read the books because they enjoy the
story, and because they find the religious themes attractive.

*I had an opportunity to see some of the letters some of your readers
sent you. They're not only inspired by your stories, but some actually
claim to having religious conversions as a result of reading your stories.*

Thousands of them. It's a wonderful thing for me to read these letters because I understand from them that the stories accomplish the purpose I had in mind for them. They do, indeed, bring people back to God's love.

When I asked him if he thought there would be any reaction if I, as he wished, stopped writing stories, Cardinal Joseph Bernardin said, "There might be some initial disappointment." But he has no sense, even though he's seen these letters, that the stories really do bring people back to God and to the church.

I don't know how to explain the psychology, but he doesn't see it, though it's in the letters, clearly. You see it in the letters; I see it; anybody that reads the letters sees it. The Cardinal doesn't.

How many millions of readers do you have?

There are fifteen or sixteen million copies of the books in print, which is, you know, a reasonable number. They get re-orders for 500,000 paperbacks every year, which is a lot of books. Of course, each one of those books doesn't get read by one reader. My guess is that the standard audience—the people that buy the books as they come out, or read a borrowed copy—is about a million and a half.

According to a survey done in the archdiocese of Seattle one out of four Catholics there said they had read my books. So I would say one out of six or one out of seven American Catholic adults are in the audience.

Do your novels have any appeal to young people?

It's fascinating to me that they do very, very well on the college campuses. I was in a meeting once at the College Booksellers Association, and they told me that the books go like wildfire. Every time I go to a college campus to autograph books, the bookstore fills up with kids. I did not anticipate that, but it delights me.

How many books have you had on the New York Times *best-seller list?*

Twelve or thirteen.

And you've had novels simultaneously on the hardcover and paperback best-seller lists?

Yes, often, often.

5

And what do you have on the best-seller list these days?

Rite of Spring in hardbound and *Patience of a Saint* in paper.

Rite of Spring *came out recently, didn't it?*

Yes. And *Patience of a Saint* came out in paperback.

So you have an audience out there waiting for your next book? And a large one, at that.

Yes, but, as the Cardinal says, there would only be some slight disappointment if I stopped writing the books at his wishes.

I meant to ask you about the response you get from men readers.

Women are much more likely to read novels than men—not my novels, but any novels—so I get more letters from women than men. But I get the same kind of letters from men as I do from women.

In fact, some of the letters I saw of religious conversions were from men.

You've grouped your novels, to my knowledge, around certain liturgical cycles or themes. Would you talk about your Passover trilogy, Thy Brother's Wife, Ascent into Hell *and* Lord of the Dance.

Each of the novels are a reflection on one of the days in the Christian Passover: *Thy Brother's Wife* is on Holy Thursday; *Ascent into Hell* is on Good Friday; and *Lord of the Dance* is on Easter. They are stories which echo the themes of the Christian Passover, which in their turn echo the themes of the Semitic Passover.

Tell us about those themes.

The Christian Passover has absorbed the fire and the water symbolisms from the pagan nature religions, where they were fertility symbols— the fire representing the male organ, and the water representing the female organ.

When the lighted candle is plunged into the water at Eastertime, it represents the consummation of the nuptials between Christ and his church. We who are baptized by that water are the first groups of this passionate union.

Now, when we grew up, we never thought of it as a sexual symbol. We would have been horrified if we'd been told that it was. There can be no doubt, however, that that's what it stands for. The old Latin said, "May this candle fructify—impregnate—these waters."

Then, you get all these overlays. First, the root of the Passover is two Semitic pagan spring festivals: the festival of the unleavened bread and the festival of the lamb, which became for the children of Israel a symbol of their covenant with God at Sinai.

Then the Christian layer on top of that is that the Passover lamb and the unleavened bread are Jesus. Then, the Romans added the fire and the water symbolism. Finally, those of us in the English-speaking world added the idea of Easter.

Where does that come from?

That's Anglo-Saxon. Easter comes from the same root word as "east," which stands for dawn, and for the East. Easter was a festival in the springtime honoring the dawn goddess who's name was Eastern, a kind of an Anglo-Saxon equivalent of the pagan Aurora.

Eastern had three symbols that always appeared with her in her ceremonies. They were bunnies and eggs and lilies. So, if you wonder where the Easter lily and the Easter egg and the Easter bunny come from, they are an Anglo-Saxon overlay. But they are quite appropriate, because they stand for life, and Easter is a festival of life, of life renewed.

How do you employ these ideas in your novels?

I'm most successful at it in the final story of the trilogy, *Lord of the Dance*, which is the Easter one. It features Noele Marie Brigid Farrell, who is a Christian goddess of spring who represents the church.

Her name Noele, Marie. . . ?

Brigid. Noele because she was born on Christmas. That, of course links Easter and Christmas, which are really the same feasts—they're feasts of the new life.

Marie because, of course, almost half of the Irish women in the world who don't have Marie as their first name will have it as their second name.

Brigid because Brigid is the Irish goddess of the dawn. Farrell is a nod to James T. Farrell's novels, which deal with the Chicago Irish a generation or two before I picked them up.

I interrupted you. You were going to show how you made the passsage from theology to story in one of your novels.

In *Lord of the Dance*, it works on many different levels. Noele actually brings someone back from the dead.

How does she do that?

Her cousin, Daniel Xavier Farrell, has been in a prison camp in China for twenty years and is assumed to be dead. She's a bit of a psychic. She gets vivid, vivid impressions that he's still alive. So, seventeen years old, she wheels and deals. Her boyfriend's father is a congressman on the Intelligence committee. He leans on the CIA, and they lean on the State Department. The State Department leans on the Chinese, and Danny Farrell is sent home.

So, it's someone coming back from the dead, a resurrection.

Is Danny appropriately exuberant?

He's not altogether sure he wants to come back. Sure, he didn't like the prison camp. He hated it, in fact. But existing in limbo or being half-dead is sometimes a lot easier than being alive. As Noele says to him at one point in the story, "Danny Xavier Farrell, resurrection isn't supposed to be easy." That's the theme: The struggle to be born again.

Then Noele discovers, to her astonishment, that Daniel Farrell isn't her cousin, but her father. She is the fruit of the passionate union between the woman who is her mother and this man that was presumed to be dead. So, she represents the church.

Do women represent the church often in your novels?

They more often represent God, but Noele is the church.

Is that the only case in which you have a woman as the church?

Noele represents the church, and the Ryan family in general in the Blackie Ryan series—that whole family represents the church, the church as a caring community.

How is that manifested?

The Ryans will take care of you even if you don't want to be taken care of. They are almost pathologically caring. Once they take you under their wing, you're under their wing, like it or not. So, in many of the stories, the people that they adopt, salvage, are reluctant salvagees.

What about Catherine Collins, the heroine of Virgin and Martyr?

She's more likely a Christ figure. She may, in some indirect way, represent the Holy Grail for Nick Curran, who pursues her, finds her, and then loses her, and then she finds herself and him too.

But she also dies a horrible death and is reborn, as Jesus is. So she might also be a Christ figure. By the way, she's reborn on her own initiative. No man saves Catherine Collins!

Some of the feminists that go after my novels, they say, "Your women are always people that need strong men to save them," and that's not true. In fact, and quite consciously and quite deliberately, my women are never saved by men. They save themselves—sometimes with men's cooperation. My women are not weak people.

You seem to do your novels in groups or series. There is the Passover trilogy, the series on the beatitudes and Time between the Stars.

The somewhat large series called Time between the Stars deals with the Ryan family, and Blackie and his relatives. The *Angels of September* is about the feast of St. Michael. *Virgin and Martyr* deals with the wintertime feasts of the two most popular non-Biblical saints: St. Nicholas and St. Catherine. Two saints, by the way, who probably never existed.

Patience of a Saint is very much a Christmas book. Redmont Peter George Kane has his religious experience in front of the green-glass skyscraper on the Feast of All Saints. The novel ends at Midnight Mass in St. Clement's church.

Rite of Spring is a spring festival. It begins on a day in May and ends on the Fourth of July. There are no particularly Catholic feasts in it, but May is Mary's month.

Angel Fire, which will be out in the spring, features the angel Gabriella, so it's about guardian angels. *Angel Fire* is a story about the presence of grace in the universe. I am not arguing theologically that my Gabriella really exists, but then I say I will be unhappy if she doesn't.

War in Heaven, which is located in 1946, is also a feast revolving around Christmas. The one I am working on now, *St. Valentine's Night*, begins on St. Valentine's morning in 1958 and ends on St. Valentine's night, 1988.

So, the books are filled with liturgical cycles and symbols and themes that seem to completely escape critics. It sails right by them. I don't think a single review of *Patience of a Saint* mentioned the fact that it begins on All Saints' Day, and that it's about how a guy becomes a saint. It's the title, it's all through the book, and they miss it—even the favorable reviewers.

Every one of your novels has a note explaining the religious—

Not quite every one of them, but I put notes in, generally speaking. That offends reviewers. You have to understand that reviewers don't like to read a whole book. So, if somebody puts in an explanation, then they attack the explanation, and they don't have to read the book. What can I tell you?

What about the science fiction books?

The science fiction books — actually there are two of them, *Godgame* and *The Final Planet*. Now, two of the other novels, *War in Heaven*, in which Blackie Ryan makes an appearance as a two-year-old, and *Angel Fire* were science fiction novellas. People said to me, about both of them, "You've got to tell us more. You've got to tell us what happens in *War in Heaven* after the young woman disappears and the suspense mounts. The naval flier in the novel finds money missing from his wallet, which means she's not a ghost, she's a live person. What happens after that?"

I say, "I don't know what happens after that."

They say, "Think about it, and tell us." So, that's how *Angel Fire* came to be written.

I don't think its accurate to call them science fiction novels. We're calling *War in Heaven* a novel, possibly a novel of the occult. *Angel Fire* we're calling a romantic fantasy, which is a fair description. It's the one out of which a movie is going to be made.

Angel Fire?

Right.

Are you doing the script on it?

No. CBS has a requirement that the author of the novel does not do the script for the TV film, which is probably not a bad idea.

Have you tried your hand at film scripts?

I've written a couple of them but have not been able to sell them until now.

When can we expect to see Angel Fire on the screen?

I would think probably sometime in 1989.

Has there been any talk of putting any of your earlier novels into movies?

Lots of talk. Some people now have an option on a daytime series, a month-long series of half-hour programs, on *Lord of the Dance*. But I don't think that will happen. Somebody actually wrote a screenplay for *The Magic Cup*, which they weren't able to sell.

The Magic Cup *is being made into an opera, isn't it?*

Yes. Father Ed McKenna, a priest of the diocese of Chicago, is writing music for it. I wrote the libretto. Next he wants to write an opera on *The Final Planet*, which should be fun.

Do you enjoy novel-writing more than writing poetry, or vice versa?

Oh, novel-writing is great fun. I like writing poetry too, but novel-writing is tremendous fun.

Do you have a theory of poetry as you do of fiction?

Not especially. Poetry is something that requires a real mood change for me. I've got to really put myself into a poetry-writing modality. Given the demands of my very busy life, that's pretty hard to do. I can write novels and answer the telephone and give interviews, or whatever. I couldn't do poetry and do that. I have to get away from things and people and sort of turn off the world, then the poetry flows.

You've written hundreds of poems.

I don't know whether there are hundreds. Scores, anyhow.

What is the role of the quest in your novels?

The quest is for the perfect love. The quest for God. Human life is a quest for God. This is not to say that the other objects or persons at which we direct our love have no value in themselves, but we seek in them for that which will only be completely fulfilled in God. They are bare hints of God, bare sacraments of God.

The quest stories are about the quest for love—the quest for lovers, and then the quest for the Lover.

Your novels are filled with symbols and symbolic imagery. Could you give us an idea of some of the things you intentionally use as symbols?

One of the favorable critics said that I layer symbols on "like Flaubert." She's right that I do layer them on. I was unaware that I was doing them like Flaubert—piling symbol on symbol on symbol.

It's always interested me that the readers seem to catch these symbols immediately. They know what they mean. They may not know they're symbols, but they know what they're about. On the other hand some reviewers, and particularly Catholic reviewers, seem to miss the symbol. They're utterly prosaic. They have no awareness of symbols at all. I don't think the symbols are particularly arcane. They are: light and darkness, good and evil, love and hatred, birth and death, renewal, the cycle of the seasons, human love. They are the sacraments, with a small "s."

Ingrid Schafer, who did a good study of your novels, Eros and the Womanliness of God: Andrew Greeley's Romances of Renewal, *also did a rather scientific survey of negative reactions to your work.*

Among priests.

What were the results of the survey?

She did it both in Chicago and nationally, and there wasn't much difference between Chicago priests and the rest.

About a third of the priests that she surveyed liked my books. They understood what they were about; they used them in their sermons; they encouraged people to read them.

Another third, some of whom had read one novel—mostly *The Cardinal Sins*—were indifferent. They didn't see the religious point to the book, but neither did they think I should be suppressed.

The final third disapproved strongly of me and my books and thought I ought to be suppressed. But only some of them had bothered to read the books.

The predictor of where people would fall on this was their attitude towards God, their image of God. If they were able to be flexible in their images of God and see God as both Mother and Father, then they tended to be favorable. If they had a narrow image of God as Father, then they were unfavorable.

The second predictor variable was attitude towards the writer—agreement or disagreement with the notion that he only writes those books to make money. Then the third was the fear that the novels would hurt the church.

If you have a rigid notion of God, if you think of the church in a rigidly institutional fashion as something that can be hurt, and if you think that the author is somebody only interested in money, then you're very likely to disapprove of the books and want the author to be condemned, even when you may not have read them.

She also did a survey among critics, didn't she?

That was a sneaky survey. She did book review editors and members of the Popular Culture Association. She had five or six passages describing sexual interludes written by a number of different novelists. She split the designs so that some of the respondents knew who the authors were, and others didn't.

The quality of my writing—it's embarrassing to report this—but the quality of the writing in my sexual scenes was rated at the top of the list by those who didn't know it was me, and at the bottom of the list by those who knew it was me.

What other writers did she include in the survey?

She had passages from Saul Bellow and John Updike, among others. Needless to say, they outclassed me when people knew who they were. But when they didn't know who they were, I outclassed them.

I'm not suggesting that I write with the same quality of writing they do. What I am suggesting is that a lot of people, including fairly sophisticated literary people, will judge my work by the fact that I, as a priest, have a reputation for writing steamy novels to make money, and not by what's actually in the text.

I have five or six quotes from some of your critics, which I would like you to respond to.

Fine.

One critic says: "For Greeley to attack the church he says he loves, to make fools of priests, portraying them as poor, pathetic, randy creatures—that's not art, that's sellout."

I never know what to make of that kind of thing because it's an utter distortion of what I do. It assumes that unless you describe everything in the church as being perfect, and every priest in it as being perfect, you're attacking the church.

First of all, readers know that everything isn't well. Secondly, in this day when a fifth of the priests have left the priesthood, when billions of dollars are lost in the Vatican's Banco Ambrosiano scandal, it is no secret anymore that the church is made up of human beings with human faults and frailties.

Moreover, the research data show that two-thirds of the readers say that the novels have enhanced their respect for the priesthood. So the critic's opinion is nonsense.

What about this: "Greeley is trying to do business both with God and Mammon at the same time."

That's somebody who is concerned that I'm making money on the books. No, I don't write the books to make money. I write them to entertain, to fascinate, to illuminate.

The word "best seller" in certain circles is a negative word. If a book is read by a lot of people and makes money, it has to be bad!

I will cheerfully acknowledge that I write my books for people, but I don't write them to make money. I am writing the stories that I like to read, and people will like to read. That is not cutting a deal with Mammon. To say that is a classic example of clerical envy—the guy who does that resents that I'm getting money and he isn't.

Another: "You won't find anyone of any literary standing who thinks his novels are worth anything."

I don't know who has literary standing. All I can say is that there have been three or four symposia on my novels by academic critics, and they've been overwhelmingly favorable. There are a couple of collections on my novels, and they are by scholars of literary standing who do think they have literary values.

You'll note, in those three statements you read, there's absolutely nothing about the content. These are all sort of smears about motivation, or sort of general purpose. Nothing about what the books say.

But go on. I like to knock these sitting ducks down.

I thought you would. Try this one: "Greeley's insistence that these are religious stories is a corruption of theology."

What can I tell you? I could say a scatological word, but I won't. You've read some of the critical essays that have been done by the scholars, and they all see the theological purposes. That particular critic doesn't see the theological purposes because he doesn't want to see them.

Finally, there's this one: "Greeley's novels wouldn't be anything if he weren't a priest."

I wonder when there's going to be a statute of limitations on that one. *Patience of a Saint* is now the ninth book in a row to make the *New York Times* hardback and paperback best-seller list. Don't you think that by now the curiosity in a novel written by a priest would have diminished?

I suspect that a lot of people were attracted to *The Cardinal Sins* by the bafflement of a priest who writes novels, but that was the only one. Moreover, it's the opposite case now: some people who have never read the books refuse to read them because they are "steamy novels by a priest."

In those novels like Ascent into Hell *and* Virgin and Martyr, *where sex becomes so demonic, what's the point you're trying to make there?*

That sex can be and often is demonic. But that it also can be sacramental. It's dangerous, but it's also wonderful, surprising, in the theological sense of those words.

In the note at the beginning of Ascent into Hell, *you make a reference to the crucifixion. How does that theme figure in the novel?*

Hugh Donlon, the hero of that story, is a guy who, all his life, lived by rules. Having failed in that, he falls apart and breaks all the rules. He discovers at the end that life isn't about rules at all; it's about responding to love with love. So, it's a Good Friday love story. It's a Good Friday story about a man who crucifies himself and then finds redemption or hope.

Does that crucifixion theme enter into your novels often?

Where ever there is acute suffering, obviously there's a cross. It enters into *Lord of the Dance*, where Noele Farrell is horribly violated. It enters into *Virgin and Martyr*, where the same thing happens to Cathy Collins. It enters, in a less horrific way, into the life of Ann Riley in *Angels of September* where she's crucified, again, by a church.

Some of my heroes and heroines are crucified by their own church. But then, they're also saved by the church, too, often by Blackie Ryan, who, as I said yesterday, represents Everypriest. They're not exactly saved by him, but he is the occasion of their saving themselves with God's grace.

Here's a quote from you, that I discovered, I believe, in Religion: The Secular Theory. *It has helped me understand something more of what you're trying to do in your novels. "Grace lurks everywhere, even, perhaps especially, in disappointments and failures."*

That's true in a number of senses. We found out in some preliminary research we've done at NORC that's going to be part of a bigger research project next year, that when you ask people what the times are that are especially important religiously to them, death—presumably, death of a loved one—is one of those that is mentioned frequently. It seems that renewal, somehow or the other, can be occasioned by death.

But I also think, in the lives of individuals, that you have to go through Good Friday before you can achieve Easter Sunday. Love has to bottom out before it can be born again. How long the bottoming out takes, how long Good Friday lasts, would differ from case to case. The movement back and forth between Good Friday and Easter is the matrix of human life and of human love.

The people I'm writing about in the present novel, *St. Valentine's Night,* their Good Friday is essentially twenty years long. So, Good Friday can be pretty long sometimes.

You refer to your novels as parables of grace. Are you trying to tell us this is what the kingdom of God is like?

Yes.

Do you think that your nonfiction writing—this is what someone said about it—is too empirical; that it does not leave enough room for God or the Holy Spirit?

Again, I am tempted to use a scatological word. The theological assumptions behind that are bizarre because they assume, quite contrary to Catholic philosophy and theology, that God intervenes outside of secondary causes—other people, things or events. Whereas, in fact, our tradition has always maintained that God's grace works mostly through secondary causes.

One doesn't want to exclude the possibility of God working directly on people. Miracles do occur. But in the ordinary course of events,

God works through the objects, the events and processes of life. I don't think any reputable Catholic theologian in the world would deny that.

So, if, then, God works through secondary causes, the secondary causes are measurable.

In what way?

You can, for example, cite statistics on the relationship between the happiness of a marriage and the frequency of prayer and say that the secondary cause of God working either through prayer or through marriage influences the other. That, you can measure.

What can we expect to see coming from Andrew Greeley's pen in the future?

God willing, more.

We've covered poetry, science fiction, mysteries, novel writing and nonfiction. Did we miss anything?

There's a book coming out a year from now called *Love Songs*, which started out actually as a treatment for a screenplay. I liked the story so much I then developed it into a novel. So, it will appear as a novel, but I don't know if the screenplay will ever be made into a movie.

The novel's about a lover who must accept forgiveness, and it's very, very difficult for her to do that. It ends on Good Friday in Blackie Ryan's room in the cathedral rectory, with Blackie taking a very small sip of Black Bushmills while winking at the medieval Madonna who presides over his room.

It's based on a theme which I used in my Holy Week sermons a couple of years ago: that it was easier for Jesus to forgive Judas than it was for Judas to accept forgiveness.

You have a really productive imagination.

Tell me about it!

I'm glad we have you.

Ah, Ron, you've got good taste.

Despite the fact that you're spread out so thin, there's remarkable productivity, and you make a contribution in every area you move into.

I'd like to curtail a lot of other things and really concentrate on the fiction and writing. This autumn I've been working on two books in the midst of airplane trips and sociological research and lectures, interviews. It's a difficult and frustrating way to work.

I would much sooner wall off the world for a good part of every day and work on the fiction, but so far that hasn't been possible. I wonder as I come to that magic number, sixty, whether I really ought to drastically realign my life so that I'm not quite spread out so thin.

II
HOME

"There's a powerful tendency in us to sanctify the
special places in our lives."

A Chicago neighborhood

Andrew M. Greeley

In your writings, you speak about your "sacred places," and you name them. They are Twin Lakes in Wisconsin, Saint Ursula's parish, Christ the King, Grand Beach in Michigan and Arizona.

Yes, that's a fair description of them.

I was wondering if we might best start off with talking about the idea of sacred places, and then talk about those sacred places in your life as kind of an introduction to who you are.

Probably it would begin with the notion that I am convinced we are "placed creatures." We are creatures with the need of a locale, simply because we're biological beings. We occupy space, and we are not rootless or nomadic creatures. We tend to settle down in a place, to make it our own, to sink roots.

Now, I say "we tend to" because, while there are propensities in the human condition in this direction, we are also remarkably plastic creatures and can become wanderers; we can become flying Dutchmen; we can move around very rapidly. Perhaps when we do it, we do some violence to our physical nature, but it's not impossible for us. We are not programmed into a specific locale like a dog is. We don't have our territory—our turf—in quite the sense that the animal would have.

We do have a tendency, when we move into a room, to put a few things of our own around the room and make it ours, to kind of leave our label on the room, so that when we come back to it, it's our place. This is the dimension of human nature that has led us to create sacred places. In the midst of things there is one spot that is the special link between ourselves and whatever keeps the cosmos going. For Russians, maybe it's the Mausoleum of Lenin in Red Square. For an Indian—a native American—maybe it's the campfire with the stones around it.

But whatever it is, there is a tendency when humans come together to find one spot of that place to be a link with the ongoing cosmic processes.

To have a special kind of place that's sacred to us, a place to which we come back when we need refreshment, renewal and revival, is natural. It's not "natural" in the sense of the old Catholic notion of natural law that everybody has to have it, but it's "natural" in the sense that there's a powerful tendency in us to sanctify the special places in our lives.

What has been the effect of the jet age on this human tendency?

One of the things that's come about as a result of jet travel is the discovery of the biological clocks in our bodies. When we violate the biological clock by going across time zones, it rebels and messes us up internally.

Studies of these biological clocks show that there is not one, or two, or three, but scores—perhaps hundreds of them—arranged in networks and hierarchies. These clocks, at least large numbers of them, are disturbed when we move around. This is evidence in the physiological sciences that we have this tendency to be rooted creatures.

These sacred places in your life, are any of them of a particular home? Does "home" add a different aspect to the idea of place?

They're "home" in some sense. I mean, Saint Angela's parish or Saint Ursula's was, of course, the place I grew up in—that's home. Christ the King was my parish for ten years. It was and still is home. Grand Beach is my house. I own the house; I live there. The same can be said of Arizona. It's a place I go. It's sort of my home away from home.

You say in your autobiography that Arizona is a healing experience for you, but it's not home.

It's not home the way Chicago is home. It's not home the way Saint Ursula and Saint Praxides and Grand Beach are home.

When you are in Arizona, do they say you are a Chicagoan when they first hear you talk?

No, Tucson is the quintessential immigrant town where there is no native Tucsonian speech. There may be a little bit from the folks that were born there, who might be 30,000 or 40,000 people, whose families were raised there. They talk a little bit Southern, but not much. So there's no special Tucsonian talk.

Can we talk about your Twin Lakes experience?

Yes.

You talk about it as having a foundational influence on you in the sense that it shaped your life. Could you tell us something about that— how it shaped your life, or why it's important to you?

It was something I always looked forward to. I loved the water, and the sand, and the woods, and the long lawns that seemed to roll down to the lake. I found it a very exciting place to go every summer. Why I found it exciting I don't know, because I certainly wasn't living in slums or anything of the sort, but it's always been a major part of my imaginative process, my dream life.

Versions of it recur in most of my novels. I don't consciously say I'm going to write about the lakes, or something like the lakes; I simply find myself writing about summer experiences.

Summer imagery has always been very, very important to me. I suppose I would say that it represents life in a very special and vibrant form—Paradise, if you will—the park, that special magic place in the summertime.

Does the lake itself have any special significance?

Oh yes! If you take the lake away, it's not summertime.

What kind of experience was the Twin Lake experience for you?

You asked, "Was the lake important?" I said that the lake was the whole thing, because if you take the lake away it isn't summer. And so, water imagery has always been important to me. It's probably no accident that I swim everyday.

We know from the religious symbols—symbols of the world religions and the history of religion—that water represents what it does represent for us in baptism: renewal, rebirth, life and life-giving power. Water represents the womb. So, it's probably the feminine imagery that also affects me. And there's a God in that symbolism that affects us in those sort of primal experiences of water as renewing.

Is that where you got the answer to your question of whether or not reality was gracious, from that experience at Twin Lakes?

No, I don't think so. I probably absorbed that through my parents. But Twin Lakes might have been the first symbolical articulation of it, or experience of it. That the lake was my first symbolization of the reality of graciousness.

You call yourself a summer person. What do you mean by that?

I love summer and I hate winter. I mean, a gray day like this is horrendously depressing. That weather and light and darkness have much more effect on me than they do on many people. So the warmth and the brightness of summertime is a powerful, revivifying thing for me, and the gloom of winter is powerfully depressing.

What's the theme, then, in your new novel, Rite of Spring? *Does it have something to do with that?*

Oh yes! It begins on a day in May, and it ends on the Fourth of July. So, it's a month in spring, turning into summer. The hero and the heroine—their friends—are on the Strand of Inch in County Kerry Island. As the book ends there are plans in their heads to go back to Grand Beach for the Fourth of July weekend.

Does summer begin the Fourth of July, or begin Memorial Day? That's a difficult question. But it begins on Memorial Day. That's when it begins unofficially, more or less. Real summer begins the Fourth of July. And, of course, it goes on the Labor Day, at least.

Summer ought to go on to Columbus Day. And this business of sending children back to school before Labor Day, indeed sometimes even in the month of August, I've always felt is a sin and a crime. It violates the sanctity of summer. Kids should not have to sit in the classroom before Labor Day.

When I signed the contract with the University of Arizona, one of my stipulations was that I would never teach the first semester as long as the first semester started before Labor Day. In Arizona, of all places! In Arizona, you know, nobody's going to think anything until the first of October!

Unfortunately, they've got to start on the 28 of August because of state laws, and all those kinds of creepy things that obsess professional educators.

How do you spend your summers?

A long time ago I said you could accomplish more work in ten months than you can in twelve, and I've always believed it. After I got the house at Grand Beach, I started to practice what I preached. I notably diminished my schedule of work. I water-ski, I swim, I sail, and I sit around and read.

Can you really manage to stick with that schedule?

To tell the truth, sometimes a lot of summer is pretty hectic, too. I fairly often cheat and work on something during the summer. Last summer, for example, the book that I have coming out from Harvard Press on religious indicators came back with requests for revisions. I should have told them to go jump in the lake, but I guess I'm not mature enough yet to tell that to Harvard Press, so I worked on it during the summer. But, I guess the big thing about summer is I don't travel—no O'Hare airport, no airplanes, no hotel rooms. I sit.

Good for you! The book on religious indicators—is that going to be a summary of your sociological work?

No, not really. It's going to be a sketch of what we know from the surveys about American religion in the last forty-five years. Fortunately, George Gallup, the elder, was a religious man. He started asking religious questions in his surveys back in the late thirties.

So, it's possible to sketch an outline of the changes and developments in American religion and in some detail. There may be some fifteen, twenty indicators for anywhere between a quarter-century and forty years—and almost fifty years for some of the items.

Did you discover anything interesting while you were working on the book?

The basic finding—and it almost prevented the book from being published, because a lot of the referees were highly critical of my ideas—is that American religious life hasn't changed much at all, at least not in its essential outlines.

George Gallup's first question was something like: "Did you happen to go to church last Sunday?" Forty percent said "yes" then, and 40 percent still say "yes."

About life after death, 72 percent said they believed in life after death fifty years ago, and 72 percent still believe that today.

So most of the indicators we have are straight lines across the page. Of course, that's not exciting—or it doesn't seem exciting to most academics. And for them it's counter-indicative because they all believe in secularization and that religion's in decline. In fact neither is true.

To get back to the Twin Lakes experience—you discovered that by hypnosis?

I rediscovered it by hypnosis. It was self-hypnosis. My colleague, Erica Fromm at the University of Chicago, the mother-in-law of my other colleague, David Greenstone, is one of the world's great experts in the use of self-hypnotism in pyschotherapy. She asked me to help her design a questionnaire, which I'm in the process of working on. She offered to teach me self-hypnotism. She thought it would help me to understand what she was up to in her project. And it turned out I was a very good subject. I was very suggestive.

What did she do?

One of the things she did was age regression—sort of bringing you down the rope ladder of your life into the depths of your childhood. You go down deeper and deeper and deeper, and you feel very, very happy. You're oh, so happy, and then you open up your eyes—your eyes inside your head—and there you are. And so I was at Twin Lakes.

Now, it wasn't that I had forgotten about that. In the biography, *The Best of Times, The Worst of Times*, that John Kotre wrote about me back in the seventies, there's a whole chapter about the Twin Lakes experience. So, it was something that I was aware of, but rediscovering it in all its vividness with Erica was very, very important. In fact, it turned me into a writer of fiction and poetry. The Twin Lakes age regression unleashed a flow of imagery that continued for weeks, and not merely in self-hypnotic exercises but in ordinary states of consciousness. Then I knew I had to write fiction.

When was that? What year was that?

It was about 1975, I should think.

And when did you publish your first novel? Your first novel was The Magic Cup. *When was this?*

Yes, *The Magic Cup* was in '79, and *The Cardinal Sins* was in '81. And, of course, *The Cardinal Sins* had in its early chapters the setting at a summer resort lake, a place that was very much like Twin Lakes except, perhaps, a little bit glamorized.

Do you still use hypnotism in your life?

Oh yes. I use it, I try to use it in my daily meditations, and I use it sometimes when I'm looking for a theme in a story or a solution to a problem in a story.

We ought to talk about your two other sacred places, Grand Beach and Arizona.

Okay.

Now, Grand Beach came into your life because you needed a place to get away?

It's a complicated matter. Cardinal Meyer, before he died, released me from full-time parish work. Bishop McDonald told me I could live anywhere I wanted. "Live in an apartment," he said. "The rectory's better, probably, but live wherever you want."

I searched. It turns out that most pastors didn't want me because they viewed me as a liability: I was a priest that would be listed as in their house and hence counted against them, but I would not be a working priest. I wouldn't, for example, necessarily be there every Sunday.

Father Gerry Scanlan at St. Dorothy's finally said, "Come and be welcome." But the place he had for me was a room and a half in a basement with frosted windows and pipes. Only if you went in the bathroom and opened the little window could you look out and see some sky. That was depressing.

So, what did you do?

So I decided I needed a place with blue sky. That was the occasion, anyhow.

But of course I had memories of Twin Lakes and summer homes. My sister says, and quite correctly, that Grand Beach is the Twin Lakes of my maturity.

Also, we had begun this community of young people who had grown up in Christ the King and had mostly left the parish because they were in college or getting out of college. It seemed that a house in the area would be a good place for that community to come together. So those are the factors that went into the decision to find a place.

But does Grand Beach have that Twin Lakes meaning for you?

Oh, yes it does.

Do you spend much of your time there?

In June I start splitting my time between Chicago and Grand Beach—a couple of days here, a couple of days there. July, I move there, but I may come into the city once a week. August, I stay there. Then, since the Cardinal won't let me do parish work in Chicago, I often go up there on weekends and say Mass there for neighbors.

So you have a community there?

Especially in the summer, there's a big community. In the winter it's smaller, but there's a community. There are people to say Mass for. It's a very important place. But because of the kinds of work I do, all I really need up there is the data bank in my twenty pound, transportable Compaq computer which I can move back and forth, so I can work up there as well as I can work here. But it is different there. It's more benign, more gracious.

Is that where water-skiing came into your life?

No, I was water-skiing before that. I learned to water-ski on vacations at Lake Geneva. I was not a teenage water-skier. I was probably thirty when I started.

I'll never forget the first time I actually got up on skis. I'd been fooling around in Lake Geneva for a week trying to learn how to ski, being towed by a boat with a 45-horsepower motor. I didn't realize it then, but it is a lot more difficult to learn with a 45-horse than with a bigger one.

So there I am, waterlogged and bedraggled, and this great big, enormous Chris Craft pulls up. This kid leans over and says, "Father Greeley, is that you? We didn't know you could water-ski." It was some kids from the parish, Mary Ellen and Patty Keene.

"Yes," I says, "I can water-ski."

"Ski off our boat!"

So they threw out a tow rope and I thought, "It's now or never." Because if Father Greeley doesn't get up and out with this boat, it's going to be all over the parish tonight. So I got up and I stayed up a presentable amount of time. And they said, "He skis pretty good for a priest."

And you got involved in wind surfing later in your life?

I have. I have.

How recently?

Two years ago.

Enjoying it?

Yes, it's lots of fun and exciting. It's exhausting, but fun. And I sail too.

You sail too? Are all your sports water sports?

Yes, I gave up golf in 1960 as bad business. The only other exercise is walking, which I like to do. Basically, I'm a water person.

Am I leaving out something about Grand Beach? Should I be asking something else that I haven't asked about its meaning in your life?

The only thing to say now is that since I don't have a parish in Chicago, it's the young people that I know up there, teenagers and young adults, who play the same role in my life that the Christ the King High Club played. About which, by the way, I should say something.

The High Club at Christ the King was about the only thing the pastor let me do, which was the most exciting part of it. The Young Catholic Student discussion groups and the summer study weeks are the most exciting kind of parish work I ever did.

What about Arizona? Incidentally, I noticed that in your list of "sacred places," all of them are local communities, except Arizona.

It's like people say "California"—but they don't mean California, they mean Los Angeles. Or in Brazil they say Bahia, which is a Brazilian state, but they don't mean the state, they mean Salvador, which is the capital of it. So, what I mean by Arizona is Tucson.

You call Arizona a healing experience.

In Chicago I was something of a square peg. The church under Cardinal Cody did not need or want me. And the university didn't need or want me. While you can say to yourself, "They're mistaken; they're wrong," it sort of accumulates on you and you begin to wonder, "Maybe I don't have anything to offer, after all." So, the welcome I received from both the church and the university in Arizona was very, very reassuring.

There's one other question I wanted to bring up—the question of your nightmares. You mentioned them in your autobiography as being very significant in your life. I almost never have nightmares.

Yes, most people don't ever have nightmares.

You have them a couple times a week?

Once a week, at least. Some weeks I have a couple. I hadn't paid any attention to them until I read an article in the *New York Times* about nightmare research in which it said that only perhaps one out of every five hundred people have nightmares every week. As I went on to read the rest of the article, it was like looking in a mirror, because it described my personality so well.

To shorten a long discussion of it, people who have frequent nightmares seem to be the kind of personalities with permeable boundaries. They absorb things. Reality flows through them, and they have quick access to the various dimensions of their own personalities. They can move back and forth inside their personas very quickly.

The way I interpret the literature on it, the nightmare is a side effect. The important thing about these kind of people is not that they have nightmares, but that the boundaries of their personalities are not rigid. They can cope with all kinds of ambiguity, obscurity and conflict rather easily—internally or between themselves and the outside world.

When you write, one of the things I'm most impressed by is your sense of self-assurance about what you're writing. Do you attribute any of that to the—

It's part of the personality type. Nightmare persons are realistic enough to know that they tend to be creative people, and they know their work is going to be criticized and they don't care. They take criticism for granted, so when it happens it doesn't bother them. The people that are really bothered by criticism are those who don't expect it. The nightmare person assumes there will be criticism and is not bothered by it.

Does that explain everything about your sense of self-assurance?

That's part of it. Also that in anything I've ever done, there's always been a considerable distance between me and the work. I don't identify myself with the work in such a way that if it's not perfect, then I'm going to be imperfect, or in such a way that if the work fails, I'm going to fail. Obviously, I'm not immune to criticism. I don't like it. It bothers me, it hurts, but it doesn't—since the work is distinct from me—destroy me. I survive it a lot more easily than many people.

It certainly sounds like it.

So, the result is that I do write with self-assurance.

The amazing thing is that you're seldom wrong.

Or as some would say, the offensive thing!

Those people that I've read who have analyzed your novels—the ones who analyze them positively—say Blackie Ryan is your persona.

In *The Cardinal Sins*, Kevin Brennan was my persona. Some of the incidents in Kevin's life have been incidents in my own life. I'm not Kevin Brennan, but my sister says I'm Kevin Brennan 20 percent of the time, and I would have liked to have been him 40 percent of the time—and much less than my Blackie Ryan. Blackie drinks Jameson's whiskey and sometimes Black Label. I don't drink. I don't drink hard liquor at all. Blackie's short. I'm not short. Blackie is a monsignor. God knows, I'm not a monsignor. Blackie is younger than I am. I'm not Blackie, though sometimes he speaks for me. But sometimes he speaks for himself. And he, like all major characters, develops a reality of his own. I can't make Blackie say something that I want him to say if he doesn't want to. What he says has to flow through his own nature. So I'm not Blackie. He's not me.

III
ROOTS

"Parents are the first and primary socializers. So I'm sure that [my parents] were, and are, the most important influence on my life."

Andrew M. Greeley with his sister, Mary Jule, and brother-in-law, Jack Durkin, and their children.

What about your parents? What influence did they have on your life?

I suppose it was enormous. Parents are the first and primary socializers. So I'm sure that they were, and are, the most important influence on my life. My Catholicism, the type of Catholicism that I'm committed to; the sense of neighborhood and place; the empiricism and the pragmatism; the distaste I have for ideology, for movements, and for enthusiasms—I'm sure I absorbed all that from my parents.

Which one had the greater influence on you? Or was there a difference?

It would be hard to say. They both read a lot. My father was something of a writer. He wrote for Knights of Columbus magazines. It would not be possible for me to sort them out. They both had a very strong influence on me.

"Lace curtain" or "shanty Irish," does that fit your family at all?

Oh, we certainly weren't shanty Irish! First of all, all the shanty Irish were on the Southside. We didn't have them on the Westside.

"Lace curtain versus shanty"—you see, they're not a dichotomy. Lace curtain conveys a certain kind of gentility and refinement which, when it's used in a negative sense, is almost a caricature. They're Irish who are trying to imitate the WASPs, or the English, the Brits in Ireland. And so, we would not have accepted either.

Now, sometimes we jokingly said we were "venetian blind Irish," which meant Americanized Irish. It was a time when everybody had venetian blinds. And then later, when I went to the Beverly neighborhood in Chicago, I was the country club Irish.

I didn't know about all those distinctions. You were born in the Depression, weren't you?

Yes, in 1928.

Did that have any long-range effects on you or your family?

Oh, it had a terrible effect on my family. My father was in the investment business and his business was wiped out. We weren't impoverished in the Great Depression. We weren't, as many people were, evicted from our homes. My father always had work; we always had food on the table; but we lost virtually everything.

My mother and father almost lost hope. The Irish had made an enormous amount of social and economic progress the decade after the War—I'm talking about World War I here—and the Depression shattered that progress. While lots of us came back after the war, my father didn't come back until 1947. There was always the fear that it was going to happen again.

And so, the tragedy of the Great Depression has always been with me. Each time a book comes out, I think, "This is the one that's going to fail." Black Monday, the stock market crash of 1987. I'm intelligent enough to realize that it's nothing at all like what happened in 1929. But it brings back too many disturbing memories.

That must have been a frightening thing. You have two sisters?

Uhm hum.

You're the only boy?

Uhm hum.

What influence did your sisters have on your life? You're the oldest child, right?

Yes. My younger sister, Mary Jule—Mary G. Durkin—who is a theologian, has had a lot of influence on my life. Much more so recently, because I've learned a lot of theology from her, a lot about the problems and the solutions that women struggle with in the contemporary world.

Emotionally?

They're family. It means they're very close. Mary Jule especially.

Were you the favorite because you were the first-born boy?

I was going into the seminary, too! Both my sisters will tell you that was I was favored by my parents, but that's calumny! They will deny that I ever had to do the dishes, and that's calumny! I certainly had to do the dishes many, many times.

Did you have a regular Catholic education, at a Catholic elementary school?

Yes. Eight years at St. Angela, and I had five years at Quigley Seminary, the minor seminary, and then seven years at the major seminary at Mundelein. So it's the requisite sixteen years of Catholic education, plus four more, which comes to twenty years of Catholic school. I was in Catholic school from my sixth birthday until after my twenty-sixth birthday.

And what did you think of your own Catholic education? Did you get a good deal?

Until the seminary at Mundelein, yes. I got a fine deal in grammar school. I didn't learn any handwriting because there were sixty people in the first grade class I was in, and I was sick for two months, and I don't think they even missed me. However, I suspect that my hand-writing would have been bad, regardless. But yes, we learned to read and write, calculate, and we learned religion. I would have no criticisms of it at all.

Quigley, the high school seminary, was a fine place. You certainly weren't made to be an intellectual. It wasn't like a British public school, or like a private school in the Northeast, but it was still a good high school, where, if you wanted to, you could learn an awful lot beyond the subjects that were routinely taught in high school.

How did you take advantage of that opportunity?

I did an awful lot of reading in high school, fiction especially, on books that would be mentioned in class, or recommended by professors.

Moreover, because it was a seminary, both the academic and the behavioral standards could be set higher than at other high schools. So that meant for a better environment for study and learning.

What did you think of seminary life?

The seminary at Mundelein was a farce. The young men and women of my generation who went to college got a much better college educa-tion than we did.

The theology training was a disgrace. It was memorizing theological manuals! And at a time when theological re-examination of the Bible was taking place in Europe and the groundwork was being laid for Vatican Council II. You heard none of that.

I could read French, so I was reading people like De Lubac and Congar and others in the original as far back as 1950. When the Vatican Council did begin, I knew the names and I recognized the ideas. I also discovered Teilhard de Chardin, the French paleontologist and mystic, at that time, though I had a most difficult time reading him.

Seminary life, was it as—let me put it this way—was it as drab as you describe it in your novels?

Oh that's what a lot of the young people ask me: "Was the seminary really like that?" and I say, "No, I thought it was worse."

That's the way it was. That's not that way it is anymore. The seminaries have changed, thank God. But they were pretty bad. It was said of our rector that he was twenty-five years ahead of his time, that he was solving the problems of 1850 with the solutions of 1875! Now, whether he was ultimately one of the best minds of the seventeenth century, I don't know.

If you had to describe seminary life in one word?

It was a disaster. It was designed to keep us in a state of permanent intellectual and emotional immaturity. The argument that would be used would be that we had to learn obedience. We weren't going to be pastors, we were going to be curates for most of our lives, and the most important virtue for the priest was obedience—not charity, but obedience! This was supposed to be training, you know, for the ministry and the priesthood in a big city like Chicago!

They taught us obedience by imposing an elaborate system of rules on us. The seminary was designed to produce immature human beings, and it did—it was successful. And it might have worked if the church hadn't changed. But, of course, the church did change. And, all of a sudden, we were expected to act maturely, and lots of us didn't. Lots of people left the priesthood in dismay.

You said about Mundelein that the laity was unimportant, that the person that counted was the pastor.

Yes, the pastor. The pastor was everything. You were a valet to the pastor. You were a serf. You did his bidding. He was God for you.

What was the basis for that kind of thinking?

The theory that went behind the seminary was that whoever was in authority represented God, and whatever he said was God's will for you. That was an unnuanced theory. I mean, you could perhaps defend that theory with a lot of elaborate nuances and clarifications. But there wasn't any clarification. You know, if the pastor said, "You go down to the store and collect my suit,"—as my first pastor would do— that was God's will. Or, "Go find my dog. He's over at such-or-such

house. Go pick him up in the car and bring him back," then you did
so. That was God's will for you. That's baloney, of course!

What inspired you to become a priest?

I often tell the story about Sister Alma Frances, the nun in eighth
grade who asked how many of us wanted to be priests. Half the guys
put up their hands, and she said, "Only one of you is going to make
it." I thought to myself, "Too bad for the others!" Actually, she was
wrong. There is one other, Bishop McNamara, out in Grand Island,
who was in that class. One of us made good—Larry is a bishop!

Now, why did you respond that way to her question?

I suppose it was the first time that it occurred to me that I could
be a priest. I liked the priests in the parish so much that the possibility of being like them, doing what they did, was enormously appealing.

Why did you like the priests?

Because my parents always treated them with great respect. It was
not servile respect. They weren't the kind of priest-worshipers that a
lot of the Irish are. My father had done some work with alcoholic priests
and so there was a lot more realism about the priests than you would
have found in some devout families.

But they did like them and respect them. And I found the priests
in the parish and their work—the group confessions, sick calls, visiting
people in hospital and helping people in trouble—I found that a very,
very appealing type of work and said, "Maybe I want to do that."

Did your parents resist or encourage your vocation?

They were mostly neutral—neutral leaning to favorable. There was
certainly never any pressure. They would have preferred that I would
have gone to an ordinary high school, instead of going to Quigley, the
minor seminary. They felt that fourteen was too young to make a
definitive decision about one's vocation in life.

I opted for Quigley because it seemed that if one went to another
high school, one would lose a year. Instead of the twelve years of study
required for the priesthood, it would take thirteen. That extra year
seemed like a long time, so I said, "No, I want to go to Quigley."

Have you ever regretted your decision?

Oh, no.

Do you attribute your becoming a priest to the fact that you are an Irish-American Catholic?

Not all Irish-American Catholics became priests. But it certainly is a vocation that was nurtured in the garden of Irish-American Catholicism. It's a very Irish vocation. What kind of vocation, if any, I would have had if I had grown up somewhere else, I don't know.

What would you have been like if you had grown up Italian-American?

I saw that question on your list and it's a fascinating one, but I can't answer it, because what I am is so much a part of the geographical, the historical and the cultural environment in which I grew up that I can't imagine myself in any other set of circumstances.

Indeed, I was thinking about that in my novel-writing. The characters in my novels, for the most part, are people that grow up in very similar environments because I can't get inside the souls of other kinds of folk. But they make some kind of appearances. I have this wonderful character in my head—she's in a short story and she's also in *The Rite of Spring*, Cindasoo McCloud, petty officer, third class, United States Coast Guard from Stinking Creek, West Virginia.

Stinking Creek?

It's a real town in a wonderful sociological study. I met a young Coast Guard woman in Buffalo, Michigan, who is the sort of model for Cindasoo, but I could never build a novel out of somebody like that. I mean, she's an Irish Protestant from West Virginia. It's beyond my capabilities of imagining what would go on inside a head like that. As a short story or a side character, fine.

So what happens to Cindasoo in your story?

Cindasoo left Stinking Creek because she wanted to see the world. She claims, with a little less than full honesty, that she's the first one in her family to leave Stinking Creek since fifty years before when that fellow Daniel Boone came through.

So, the Coast Guard sent her to Michigan City, Indiana. Blackie Ryan says to her, "Cindasoo, is Michigan City any better than Stinking Creek?" And she says, "Yes, priest, it is, but not much."

Have you known women to whom you could have been happily married?

Yes, some.

Is there something absent in your life because there has not been a long-term relationship with a woman?

Sure. And there's something present in my life because I've been a celibate. So there are assets and liabilities to both commitments.

Who are your heroes?

My heroes? Cardinal Meyer was certainly a great hero. Jack Shea, the author of *Stories of God*, is a hero; Leo Matthews is a hero. That's three priests. Pope John XXIII was a hero. Ed Monahan was a hero.

In your autobiography you identify yourself with Don Quixote.

I say people identify me with Don Quixote. They think I tilt at windmills and maybe I do. Maybe I get into conflicts that I ought not to get into.

But my most Quixote behavior is writing novels. That's really tilting at windmills for a priest—to suddenly sit down and start turning out novels, popular novels that acknowledge there are sexual attractions between men and women.

I had a note the other day from a priest who said reading my autobiography was a tremendous liberation for him because all his life he had suffered guilt because he found women's bodies attractive. It was an intelligent letter. I don't think he was an intellectual clergyman, but he wasn't dumb either. Somehow or other he had been trained to believe that finding the bodies of women attractive was evil.

That's tragic. If it's not Don Quixote, what is the image, the character, that best describes you? How would you describe yourself?

There are two kinds of characters, mythological characters, which certainly keep coming up in my novels. One is Ulysses, the man who goes away and comes home. And the other is the Lancelot, Galahad or Parsifal, or in the Irish version of it, Con MacArt, the quester searching for the Grail.

Blackie Ryan, is he the one that's most closely modeled on a priest that you know than any other of your fictional characters?

Monsignor Monty Brennigan, who appears in many of my novels, is modeled on Monsignor Diggie Cunnigham. Diggie, who is ninety-four now, knows this and is immensely flattered. Then, MacNamara in *Lord of the Dance* is modeled on a Chicago priest named Dick Dempsey, who is also a Navy chaplain.

Blackie is modeled on a real-life priest, who is not in the Chicago diocese. His name is Jimmy Mahoney. He's a priest in Jersey—and we'll have to see whether Jimmy minds that being mentioned in this book! He looks like Blackie, he talks like Blackie, and he thinks like Blackie.

Sometimes, though, what Blackie says would not be what Jim would say or what I would say, but sometimes he's my spokesman. He tends to say my ideas the way Jim would say them. There's a line, the opening line in the novel I'm working on now, that goes like this, "I hated this place when I was here. I've hated it ever since I left and I still hate it." Then the second line is, "The little priest lifted his near-sighted eyes and said, 'There's lots of ironies in the fire.' "

What's the name of this forthcoming novel you mentioned?

This one is called *St. Valentine's Night*, and I've finished about thirty pages.

What was your most important existential or personal discovery in your lifetime?

I guess the most striking one was discovering at some stage in the game, about 1960, that people liked me. That was a remarkable discovery. I still haven't quite completely accepted that. Then, more recently, the discovery that I could write stories that people like to read.

IV
PARISH

"A priest in a parish he likes and where he is liked
is very much like a man in love."

Andrew M. Greeley enjoys his beloved Chicago skyline from a boat on Lake Michigan.

What was life like as a parish priest in your early days?

It was terrifically exciting. I've been for the last several months reading the chapters of Father Leo Mahon's memoirs as they come out of his typewriter. They're very, very interesting.

Leo and I are basically the same kind of person. We grew up on the Westside of Chicago. He's more street people than I am because he's the son of a policeman.

He compares the relationship between a priest and his parish to a love affair. That is an excellent metaphor. A priest in a parish he likes and where he is liked is very much like a man in love.

Were you ever caught up in this kind of love affair?

I was caught up in a love affair with Christ the King, which has never ended. I was out there the other night for the thirtieth reunion of the first class I had in the sixth grade, the class of 1957, and it was a marvelous experience. It's still very much a part of me, my life.

Was there anything special about that love affair?

To make the love affair even more acute, it was and is a special neighborhood. The neighborhood had a forest preserve in the north and two golf courses in the east and a railroad track on the west and on the east, so it's isolated from the rest of the city. Curving streets, hills, trees and big homes. A lovely place physically. It was also small, so intense community was possible there. A lot of its Catholics had grown up together in other neighborhoods and migrated there about the same time. So it was magic, psychologically, and still is.

Was it a multi-ethnic parish?

Yes, it was Irish!

That's a good question, because, of course, it wasn't. When I was there, it was only half Catholic. If you looked at the data, that's what it was. But everybody in the parish thought it was 90 percent Catholic. They were singularly unaware of the existence of the others. Sunday afternoons they used to play softball in the public square, a Protestant ''public''—because most of your Protestants went to public school—softball game on one corner and a Catholic softball game on another corner. Outfielders occasionally passed one another. There wasn't any fighting, but there wasn't any conversation, either. It was two completely different worlds, and at that time they were hostile.

Now twenty years before, when the Catholics began to move in—the neighborhood had been there almost since the end of the century—there were some crosses burned on the St. Barnabas's front lawn and things like that, so there was some conflict. By our day there wasn't any conflict. While most of the Catholics were Irish, there were some Germans, Italians and Poles.

What marked them was not so much ethnicity as social class. It was one of the first college-educated parishes in the archdiocese, populated by professionals—doctors, lawyers, dentists. There were some really affluent people, but they would be businessmen or construction contractors or folks who had inherited wealth. Most of the parish was made up of simply very successful professional people.

What was church life like?

We had a brand-new church, a modern church going up on Hamilton Avenue, as I arrived. The pastor, for all his faults, as it seemed to me then anyway, was much better than most of his generation. We had the Mass of the Day every day—you were a flaming liberal if you had a Mass of the Day instead of the Requiem Mass. He also tolerated Cana Conferences, the Christian Family Movement (CFM), all those kind of groups—which again, in the middle fifties, looked like the hope of the future of the church.

What are some of the fondest memories you have of parish life? Some of the things you really—

The pastor really didn't trust his associates. He had founded the parish. It was his; they were his people. He was jealous of it. He was terribly afraid that his curates would take it away from him, that they would become closer to his people and replace him in their affection. He would not even let us stand in the back of the church to talk to people on Sunday mornings.

It was worse than that. The last two Masses, the 11:15 and the 12:15, would have more than half the people in the parish at them, and he wouldn't let us say those Masses. He would bring in Carmelite monks to say them, so that the majority of the people wouldn't even hear us on Sundays. So, he really tried to keep us away from lay people whenever he could.

I put up with that for ten years. God forgive me, I can't believe, looking back on it, that I accepted that.

How did you keep in touch with the lay people?

CFM was a strange exception. He'd let us go into people's homes for CFM meetings. Because that was going on in other parishes, you know.

For the most part, the only people he trusted me with were the teenagers, whom he despised. But he figured he had to do something for the teenagers, so I was made the teenagers' priest—a job for which I felt I had no qualifications. I had never been a teenager, God knows. And I knew nothing about working with them. Nothing at all. I was scared stiff.

But, somehow, it worked. I don't know whether I had a natural immaturity that even to this day makes it possible for me to relate to kids very easily. Any priest that can relate to young people after he's forty is either weird or has special gifts of nature and grace.

You didn't get along with your pastor too well then.

Heavens, no. He was so suspicious of us. When I got there in the first summer, he decided since there wasn't really much to do—the parish closed down in the summer—we would take the parish census. So I was sent out to do the parish census, but only during the daytime; if I went around at night, they would offer me drinks and he didn't want that. He warned me many, many times about keeping the five-year rule.

What was that?

We weren't supposed to drink for five years in Chicago, because Cardinal Mundelein thought, "If I can keep them sober for five years, then I don't have to worry." That was demonstrably and empirically false, but it was still the premise upon which the diocese worked. Keep them sober for five years.

I kept saying, "I don't drink. I'm never going to drink much. It's not going to be a problem." The pastor didn't want me out on the streets in the evenings.

So that meant, of course, that the only people I would get to know while taking the census would be the women and the children. He did not seem to fear that I would get involved in any love affairs with the women; he was afraid I would drink with the men.

You have renewed your relationship with the people in that parish in recent years, haven't you?

No, with the people in that parish, the relationship never ended. I still see lots of close friends. Many of them. I've renewed the relationships with the people with whom I grew up in St. Angela's or St. Ursula. Those are the relationships that have flourished again.

Did St. Angela's have a formidable influence on you?

Oh sure! Because that was the parish of my childhood. That's where I encountered the church as an institution—the priest, the nuns, the ceremonies, the liturgies, the rituals of the parish school, all of which are celebrated in my fiction.

We were doing dialogue mass in the mid-thirties! That doesn't seem like much now, but in the mid-thirties, it was something else. While some of the nuns were troubled persons, it was not an oppressive school. Nor were the various pastors oppressive people. I believe the horror stories that I read and hear about what priests have done and still are doing, but it was a very benign parish in which I grew up and there were no horror stories.

It was a place where things happened and where the priests were friendly and the nuns—at least many of them—were nice. I often ask myself when I write—I'm working on a series of books now about a guy named O'Malley, who in my imagination graduated from St. Angela the same year I did—I ask myself if I'm romanticizing it. I don't think so. I've caught what it was like.

How can you be sure about that?

I've had some of my recovered friends from that era go through the books, and they say, "That's what it was like!"

It was a nice place. The institutional church in my formative years was always a nice institution. Not until I got to the major seminary did I see the bad side of it. Of course, I've seen plenty of the bad side since, but that doesn't outweigh those formative years where you had good priests, good nuns, a good school and a good parish.

So you wouldn't be of the opinion that the parish is passé.

No, on the contrary. The difficulty with the parish is that the people and the staff don't realize what a marvelously ingenious human institution it is, particularly if it has a school. It's one of the great, all-time community-reinforcing institutions human ingenuity ever developed.

People have a hunger for community and they do everything they can to create neighborhood institutions, though they might not use those terms, and the parish church has got enormous possibilities for community generation. Unfortunately, with some exceptions, like my friend Monsignor Tom Cahalane, I don't think the clergy see the possibilities of making the parish a community center. Nor do they realize how important the parochial school is in this structure of the parish community.

So, as far as parishes being passé, the parish may for different reasons be even more important in the suburbs than it was in the old inner city.

I agree with you. So how do you get that message out to the folks?

I don't know. I've done my best for thirty years, and still people keep saying, "Well, the parish isn't important." That's nonsense, nonsense. The change is that the leadership in these parishes is not as responsive to people's needs. Now maybe the needs are more complex and elaborate, but the people still need a school, they need a church, they need a priest for the sacraments, they need some place to go, they need a center for their lives.

That's pretty simple, and lots and lots of immigrant pastors had created such parishes. The suburbs are more complicated and I think that, with some exceptions, we are missing all kinds of urban opportunities.

Take a look at this archdiocese of Chicago. The thirty or forty fringe parishes that go around the rim of the city, that are the heart and soul of the diocese—most of them are disaster areas—conflicts between priests and people. They are populated by priests—insecure priests, frightened priests, priests who think that to be a pastor means to be authoritarian—that have no sense of who their people are. I'm appalled by it and astonished that people continue to hang in there, but they do so because they figure it's their parish as much as the pastor's.

You still do parish work in Arizona?

Yes, I work in four parishes.

Four? How do you do that?

I alternate between two parishes on regular weekends. I do one parish one weekend and another the next weekend. On Wednesdays during

Lent and during Holy Week, I go up up to the Catalina Mission in the mountains.

One Sunday a month I go to Mary, Mother of Sorrows, which is the parish of my friend, Monsignor Tom Cahalane. It's a very special parish. I like it. It's very enjoyable. These are different kinds of parishes, different kinds of people, different kinds of priests, and it's fun.

And the teaching?

The teaching I enjoy very much, though it's hard work. Now with the royalties from my books, I've taken myself off the faculty payroll. So they don't pay me. They haven't paid me for a number of years. So I can teach when I want and what I want.

I normally teach one class a semester in sociology and religion. It's pure fun. I enjoy the classroom enormously. I'm exhausted at the end of it. But I intend to continue teaching out there as long as they will have me. Though in truth, and it's kind of strange, what keeps me there now is the parish work.

Really?

Yes. I went to Arizona because I needed an academic base. I don't need an academic base anymore. But I stay there, even though it's hard not to deal with Chicago, I stay there because I can do parish work there.

Why can't you do parish work in Chicago?

I'd have to stop writing the novels. That was Cardinal Joe Bernardin's terms, "Stop writing the novels, I'll let you do parish work."

Has he read your novels?

Oh, I don't know. He may have—he read *The Cardinal Sins,* I know that, but that's irrelevant. What he thinks of them doesn't matter; he gets complaints. One complaint cancels out a thousand favorable letters.

Jim Roach, his Victor General, told me I'd have to do public penance for the harm done by the novels. Bernardin said to me later on that he personally didn't think public penance was an appropriate thing at all.

But I said, "Whatever you call it is not important, you want me to stop." He said, "I will feel better if you did." He's absolutely intractable. It doesn't matter how many books or articles are written, or the research I've done on the readers or the tons of positive letters, it's the complaints that count. I suspect he gets some from the Vatican as well.

You think he has a right to ask you to stop writing novels?

Sure he has a right to ask. He can't order it—he wouldn't order it—but he has a right to ask. It is a foolish request because it lets a bishop become a victim of the lowest common denominator of clerical envy.

Most of the people that complain haven't read the books, or if they're a bishop they've read a page or two pulled out of context. If you let such people blackmail you and not support a priest, the effect of whose work is clearly established now, you're a coward.

You titled your autobiography, Confessions of a Parish Priest. *Despite the fame from your sociological research and your novels, do you still consider yourself a parish priest?*

Sure. Mark Harris profiled me in an article in the *New York Times* magazine. In it he said that after he read all the letters that I receive because of my novels, he agreed I was a parish priest, and that my parish was in the mailbox. That says it very well.

V
UNIVERSITY

''You got your doctorate in record time?''
''Twenty months.''

Andrew M. Greeley

Mission San Xavier, Arizona

How did you get started at the University of Chicago?

A friend of mine from the seminary, John Crean, left after a term in philosophy and went to that university to study sociology. He kept in touch with me, and on vacations I would go out there and meet him and some of his fellow students. I even met some of the faculty members. That stimulated my interest.

I remember saying to Cardinal Stritch when he saw me before ordination that I might like to study sociology some day, and he made a note to that effect. So, even then, I had begun to think about sociology.

When I was sent to Christ the King, the concept of social class really began to become important to me because I was dealing with a different social class than I expected. We'd been trained in the seminary to deal with immigrants and the children of immigrants—basically working class, "cap and sweater people" as one of my pastors called them. Well, at Christ the King we had college-educated professionals.

So, it seemed to me then that sociological models and theories would be enormously important in helping us plan how the church was going to respond to this new social environment that a college-educated population was going to create for us.

Is this when you began writing?

I began to read the books, first. David Reisman's *The Lonely Crowd* was an especially important book because it was concerned with the suburbanization of America. While Beverly wasn't quite a suburb politically, it was certainly a suburb geographically and culturally.

So I began to devour sociology books and to meet again with people from the university.

My first two books which were published at that time, in the late fifties. *The Church in the Suburbs* and *Strangers in the House* were really pop sociological considerations of the challenge for the church in dealing with the colleges and the kid population.

What do you think of those books today?

When I was doing my autobiography I glanced through those books again and found nothing to disagree with. The problems I foresaw and laid out are still valid.

I'm really disappointed that the church has not adjusted to the fact that it's no longer an immigrant, working-class institution. You don't have to argue it anymore. People accept the fact that they have college-educated parishioners, but the pastoral ministry in the church and the institutional organization of the diocese simply do not take into account the demographic and educational changes.

Was there any resistance from either hierarchy or clergy to your getting your doctorate?

No, quite the contrary. When Cardinal Meyer came to Chicago, he called me down to the chancery to tell me he'd read my books and liked them and wanted me to keep on writing. In 1959 that was an incredible thing. Here you have a bishop calling you in, not to tell you to stop writing, but to tell you to continue to write. That was one more gracious experience. St. Angela and Quigley Seminary had been gracious, and now this was graciousness from a very special kind of bishop.

Did he have anything else to tell you?

He said, "Stay in touch with me. If there's anything you think I should read before it's published, you need to inform me or to warn me."

So, in the summer of 1960 I brought in the manuscript—maybe it was the gallies—from my second book, *Strangers in the House*. It was a series of reflections on Catholic teenagers in the suburbs. It was then that I asked him about graduate studies in sociology.

His response was instantly favorable. "Oh yes," he said, "that really ought to be done." Then he said, "We don't have enough priests now," which was nonsense. We had plenty of priests, but he had been led to believe that we didn't have enough priests.

So he added, "I don't think I can spare you full time, but would it be possible for you to continue at Christ the King and go on to graduate school? At Loyola, for example?"

I said, "Well, it would be if you told the pastor that you wanted me to do it. Otherwise, it would not be possible."

"Loyola or the University of Chicago?" I asked.

"Oh yes," he said, "that's a lot closer to Christ the King, isn't it?"

I said, "Yes, it is."

So, on sheer geographical grounds I was sent, not to Loyola, but the University of Chicago, by the Cardinal. And while my pastor was offended because he was losing a priest part of the time, the Cardinal said he wanted it, so that's the way it was. He heard confessions for me Saturday afternoons so I could study.

The Cardinal?

The pastor. It would have been more remarkable for the pastor to do it than for the Cardinal.

So that's how I came to go to graduate school. I applied to both Loyola and to Chicago. It took Loyola a semester to admit me; Chicago admitted me on the spot and I never left.

You got your doctorate in record time?

Twenty months.

That's incredible.

And foolish, too. But I had no idea what the Cardinal had in store for me, so I figured I didn't have much time.

Looking back, he would have given me all the time I wanted, but I wanted to get it out of the way to be prepared. Also, he had nothing particular in mind for me. He wanted me to get the doctorate in sociology. I was told later that he wanted me, after I got the degree, to become part of his household and, I guess, teach him sociology at the supper table. Of course, he died before that happened. But that would have been an interesting career path.

Your dissertation?

It was on the career plans of Catholics. At that time, there was a lot of lamenting and gnashing of teeth about the failure of Catholics to pursue academic careers, particularly careers in the sciences. Father John Tracy Ellis, the church historian, had a book on it at Doubleday. It was all about the academic failures of American Catholics.

I learned about a project underway at NORC in 1960-61, a study of 30,000 graduates, people who had graduated in June of '61. Jim Davis, who had been one of my teachers, was directing the project, and so I saw the possibility of a dissertation. With 30,000 students, there'd be a lot of Catholics, and I could find out a lot about them.

We knew almost nothing, at that time, sociologically about Catholics. I talked to Father Bill McManus, who was then the superintendent of schools in the Chicago archdiocese. I said, "Bill, if I do this, what should I focus on?" He said, "For the love of God, find out why our kids don't go to graduate school."

What were the results of your investigations?

I will never forget the first finding. It was a cross-tab of plans of college graduates for their next year by religion, ground out of an old 101 counter-sorter. I came into the office on Saturday morning to pick it up, and Jim Davis had written across the top of it, "It looks like Notre Dame beat Southern Methodist this year, because the Catholic students were more likely to apply to graduate school."

So there had been a social change. I guess at this stage of the game social change is acknowledged, but, boy, the Catholic left really resisted it then.

How did they react?

There was a symposium in *Commonweal* attacking me and my work. I was called a naive optimist and accused of wanting to be a bishop. But all I was doing was simply reporting the facts. The facts were, "Yes, Catholics were going to graduate schools. Yes, they were choosing academic careers. And the Catholics going to Catholic schools were even more likely to do this."

The facts were not being evaluated as facts; they were being evaluated as statements and opinions, value judgments and efforts of mine to feather my own ecclesiastical nest.

That began a long war between me and the academic establishment in *Commonweal*. They've falsified everything I've done ever since, and I still can't understand it. There was a terrible, terrible resistance on the part of the Catholic left to the fact that American Catholics were catching up. Now, Catholics are one and a half times as likely to graduate from college as other Americans.

You mean that battle is still going on?

Every once in a while that comes up again and somebody laments that the Irish, for example, have not really made it to the upper middle class or they're not as well-educated as other Americans or not as successful, and that's baloney. But the self-hatred, what Father Ed Duff called the mass masochism of the Catholic liberals, has not really died completely.

Was it before or after your dissertation that you got involved with the National Opinion Research Center (NORC) and the study of American pluralism?

I began my involvement with NORC in June of '61, when I dropped into Davis's office to participate in the study, because it was an NORC project. I haven't left since.

Then the next thing we did, Peter Rossi and I—Rossi was the director of NORC—was a study of the Catholic population in the United States, focusing on the effects of Catholic schools, which was a gold mine. It was the first full-blown sociological study of American Catholics, and it was funded by the Carnegie Foundation. We put an ethnic question into the survey.

Why?

My interest arose from the fact that in Chicago ethnicity mattered. Ethnicity was part of the warp and the woof of life in the city, and to deny its importance was absurd. So I really got involved with ethnicity because I was convinced it was an important factor in our lives and that sociologists were, for ideological reasons, ignoring it.

What did they think about it at NORC?

Pete Rossi was very sympathetic to the idea. He said the only strain he and Alice had in their marriage in the early years was at the dinner table. He thought dinner was for talking, and Alice, who was German, thought that dinner was for eating. It took them a long time to figure out why they were always fighting at dinnertime. So that's how I got into ethnicity.

Why did you ever decide to leave Chicago and go to Arizona?

I had always said that there were only three sociology departments in the country that could attract me: Harvard, because they never had a Catholic, much less a priest, in their sociology department; The City University of New York, because at that time it had distinguished chairs and New York City; and Arizona, because it had a very distinguished sociology department, and because I used to go out to Scottsdale in the wintertime for a week of R and R and I liked it.

The City University of New York offered me a distinguished professoriate and then withdrew it at the last minute when the city tottered on the edge of insolvency. Then Arizona, in the person of my old friend Stan Luberson, began to recruit me. I did not really take it seriously. I went out because it was a free trip to Arizona. I laid down all kinds of impossible conditions which they cheerfully met. So my bluff was called.

After my unfortunate experience at the University of Chicago, it seemed to me that a position at Arizona would also wipe the records clean. If you're good enough for their sociology department, you're good enough for any department anywhere.

Also, I had been playing the grantsman game for too long. I was tired of the endless, usually fruitless, trips to New York and Washington to get funded for research. An academic base would be a very different sort of thing.

What was your most important sociological discovery?

The most important one is the one in my recent book for Harvard Press about the continuity of religion in America: religion in America has hardly changed.

Focusing that down more narrowly, the ability of American Catholicism to survive the changes made by Vatican Council II has been remarkable. We lost lots of priests and nuns, but we didn't lose many lay people at all. The birth control issue had instant impact on church attendance and a long impact on institutional credibility, but it didn't cost us many people. They didn't leave the church.

The defection rate, when I began my research in 1960, was 12 percent, 12 percent of those born Catholic were no longer Catholic. Now, you take the change in the age composition of the population into account, and it's only 13 percent. That's an astonishing achievement.

I sometimes think that the clergy, all the way up to the Vatican, have done everything we could in the last twenty-five years to drive people out of the church. They haven't gone, and they're not going to go, and that's astonishing.

But isn't one of your points also that the nature of their commitment to the institution has changed?

Yes, though I'm not so sure that the change is perhaps as great as it may seem. They've now elected to be Catholic on their own terms. But that would have happened anyhow with the increase in educational achievement. The people's definition of loyalty is no longer blind obedience.

Has the church been responsive to needs you see for social science research?

One of the things that frosts me most about theologians and church authorities is their babble about the human sciences. Take, for example, this wonderful new series of books on the liturgy that's come out through St. John's in Collegeville. The writers are all talking about human sciences and about sociology that they don't take seriously.

I said to one of them: "Hey, if I was talking about Scripture and I was citing a book that denied the synoptic hypothesis, you wouldn't want anything to do with me. You'd think I was crazy. Well, you're playing the same game when you selectively pull books from my profession and don't pay any attention to what the mainstream of the professionals are doing."

Most talk among the theologians or the church leaders about the human sciences is happy talk. It's pious babble. It is not a respectful consideration of the human sciences.

VI
NEIGHBORHOOD

"When people move into new communities, they immediately try to set up ties, which is the essence of what a neighborhood is."

Andrew M. Greeley

Popular popcorn shop

What about neighborhoods? Are they sacred places?

Gerry Suttles, a sociologist who has, perhaps, done more work on neighborhoods in recent years than anybody else, has two things to say about neighborhoods. First of all, they're places to be defended because they're projections of the self. Then, secondly, they are those spots on a checkerboard of a city where you're important, not because of what you do, but because of who you are.

At least for some people, some more than others, those kinds of communities are, indeed, sacred. Some can leave their neighborhoods with the greatest of ease. Some leave them with great sadness.

What picture do you have in mind when you think of a neighborhood?

I think of St. Ursula's and St. Praxides.

The name St. Praxides is a funny story. I had no idea who St. Praxides was. None. But it was a name that had been stuck in my head from the reading of the martyrology at the seminary. So, when I first began to do memos to myself about an upper-middle-class, professional parish back in the fifties, Christ the King obviously, I called the parish St. Praxides. Then, as the myth grew in my novels I had to make up stuff about St. Praxides. So, I said that St. Praxides was the woodsman who chopped down the trees from which were made the boat that St. Christopher used to come back across the river, after he carried the baby Jesus to the other side. So, in my novels, in the back of St. Praxides's church, there is a picture of St. Praxides, a great, big, stained-glass image of St. Praxides striding through a forest with his axe in his hand.

But it turns out that the real St. Praxides is a she, not a he. Her job was to mop up the blood of the martyrs off the floor of the arena. A typical picture of St. Praxides is of this young woman with a towel, a blood-stained towel, having wiped up the floor.

So, in the book I'm working on now, *St. Valentine's Night*, we have to change the whole image. I don't know how I am going to get away with this. I think I'll brazen it out and not even try to explain.

What is the neighborhood at its best?

It's best as a place where you come home to to be renewed. It's a place where you matter. It's a place where you're important because people know you and they know your family. It's a place where you're loved.

Why do neighborhoods figure so prominently in your novels?

Because I am so much of a neighborhood person. I still identify with them. I celebrate them. I think they are terribly important institutions. Moreover, the kinds of people I know and understand are neighborhood people, so, of course, they would have neighborhoods.

Where is that best put forth in your novels? Or is it in all of them?

It's in some more than others. In *Lord of the Dance*, of course, set in St. Praxides. In *Ascent into Hell* set in St. Ursula's. In *The Cardinal Sins*, it's St. Ursula's too.

It would be hard to find a novel of mine in which there isn't a neighborhood. Even in *The Final Planet*, a recent science fiction novel, the spaceship Iona is a neighborhood.

Your novels are basically about six neighborhoods, I think.

Yes.

Are you going to run out of stories for those neighborhoods?

I haven't yet. *St. Valentine's Night* is about a TV reporter, enormously successful, a great, great television communicator, who comes back to a neighborhood, a place he hates, for a class reunion, and gets all swept up in it again. He comes back, and discovers, in its own way, it's even more dangerous than the Hindu Kush mountains in Afghanistan.

If neighborhoods are such wonderful places, why is our society bent on destroying them?

I think the kinds of people who are bent on destroying them are people who either don't have any roots or have suppressed their own roots and look at neighborhoods as obstacles to the rational planning of our city. That would include city planners, university professors, folks like that.

Government has the same attitude to neighborhoods?

Yes, I think so. The kinds of court decisions, for example, about neighborhood schools, which were maybe well motivated in terms of their positive racial effect, were nonetheless savage blows to neighborhoods. Once you start bussing kids out of neighborhoods, parents have less loyalty to the neighborhood, and they're likely to move out of the whole school district. The bussing decisions have been disastrous for neighborhoods.

Most of the public housing legislation, and the way the legislation applies, disregards neighborhoods completely.

In the media, too, there's the bias or the bent that the neighborhood is something that's vanishing, and that perhaps it ought to be vanishing. They think it's a relic of medieval religion and things like that.

I agree. The neighborhood is a relic of medieval religion. The neighborhoods I know transplanted most of Ireland's religion. But that doesn't mean that they're bad, or that they're vanishing.

You don't think they're vanishing?

No.

Do you have the data to back that up?

There is evidence that when people move into new communities, they immediately try to set up ties, which is the essence of what a neighborhood is. Yes, I think there's evidence of that.

There is mobility, of course, but people usually move either within the same neighborhood or to the next neighborhood over. People, when they move, don't move very far, unless they're in the upper elitist society. It's only those in the the national professional system that make big moves.

I quote from Andrew Greeley. You said, "You can ignore neighborhoods, destroy them, obliterate them, but beware, they will spring up somewhere else."

That's what they do.

Why?

Because we are creatures of place, and we are creatures that require social ties. So, where place and social networks come together, the first thing you know, you've got a neighborhood.

And that's the reason people get attached to neighborhoods?

Yes, and then your kids play with the kids down the street, and you get to know the people down the street. Pretty soon, you have a neighborhood organization.

And geography is important to human beings, you're saying? To being human?

Yes. For example, as I said earlier, we are sufficiently plastic creatures that we can act for a short time as if our biological clocks didn't exist; we can move around a lot more than might be best for us. But we move around a lot at the price of putting a severe strain on our relationships with our spouse and our children.

It is not good for the family to move a lot as a unit, either. National moves from one end of the continent to the other tend to have a fairly negative effect. It's easy enough to move kids when they're little, but once they get into junior or senior high, moving around the country has a terribly bad effect on them.

I think lots of moves notably affect the relationship between a husband and a wife. To tell you the truth, I have not tried correlating mobility with divorce, but I bet there's a correlation there that's pretty strong.

Usually, on scales that list events that cause the most stress, moving is way up there, first, second or third.

Large corporations don't seem to take that seriously. They move their personnel around like they're checkers on a checkerboard without any consideration of the impact that they will have on people's physiological and pyschological lives.

I think that's true of church too—this crazy notion of moving a priest every six years! If the parish is a love affair, how many broken love affairs can you go through before you burn out?

You get terribly involved with your first parish, but six, seven years comes along, and they move you. On to the second parish—you do the same thing. Then, they move you, and it's even more damaging, if anything. So, you get to the third one, and you decide to cool it so that the pain of separation won't be as much.

Anything we know about psychology suggests that this is very unwise. But still the diocesan personnel boards around the country proceed ahead with that. They'll say, "It's good to move people." How do you know it's good?

Your friend, the sociologist, Gerry Suttles—once, you quoted him as saying, "Neighborhood is, by definition, a place to be defended." What does that mean?

He means it's an extension of home and family. Defend the neighborhood because, by so doing, you are defending your own hearth.

In what sense is the term "old neighborhood" a religious term?

The old neighborhood, of course, is the place wherein the first generation settled and the second generation grew up and maybe where the third generation was born. So it's always the place where you came from. It's always the place where you're from.

Is it a religious term? If we call it the old parish, it might be. But, you see, for us urban ethnics, neighborhood and parish mean the same thing. Meet somebody in Tucson and they say, "Oh, I'm from Chicago." Then ask them "Where in Chicago?" and they tell you the parish.

Is suburbanization killing neighborhoods?

I don't think so—certainly not in this diocese, in this urban area. If anything, in my experience, a suburban neighborhood's ties to its parish are even stronger. If anything, they have a broader spectrum of services for their people, and the people expect more of the parish.

If neighborhoods disappear, what would be the loss to America?

We would lose an important segment of our social structure. The neighborhood is an institution around which much of our lives get organized. It's impossible to have society without neighborhoods. European urban areas are something like neighborhoods, but I don't think they're as intense as many, many American neighborhoods are.

Neighborhooding seems to be what you have now in the lofts of Greenwich Village, the high-rises of Manhattan and around here, too, in downtown Chicago. There are a lot of folks that say this area here with it skyscraper apartment buildings is becoming a neighborhood. Halsted Street where all the yuppies live is beginning to be a neighborhood, too.

In our society, anyway, there's a strong propensity to create these intense local communities.

What do neighborhoods have to do with roots or belonging?

They're another way of saying the same thing. When I say that we humans need neighborhoods, I mean we humans need something to belong to, we need a place to sink our roots, even if it's only for a short period of time. It's the need for the familiar. We are animals, placed creatures, and we like familiar places.

Let me give you another quote from Andrew Greeley. You say, "Freedom is ultimately facilitated by having roots, by having a place to call home, by having a group to which one belongs." That sounds contradictory.

It can often be, of course, because there is a tendency for intense communities and for neighborhoods to be restrictive. Parishes can be, too.

You asked me earlier when the parish was at its best; you didn't ask when the parish was at its worst. At its worst, the parish can be like Salem, Massachusetts, in the time of witchcraft trials. That kind of parochialness is a very serious temptation to a parish.

But it is also possible for the neighborhood to be the ground on which you stand, your base of operations; a place where you have your own social location and self-definition. A place out of which you work.

And you need that to be free?

It's a big help. Because, you see, if you have a place like that, there are a lot of decisions you don't have to be bothered by every day. You don't have to rethink your position every morning. You know who you are and where you come from, and that's a big help. It facilitates a lot of other decisions.

But I thought a free person was someone who cut all his or her ties?

That's what American graduate school education tries to persuade you to think: that the only free man or woman is the alienated one. That's, of course, nonsense. Alienation is not freedom; it's chaos. The alienated person, the rootless person, the person who is cut off from everything, is, if not mad, then at least has to decide again every day who he or she is, and where they come from.

About racism in the neighborhood you say that it is present and mixed inextricably with other problems of changing neighborhoods. Yet, if financial panic and fear of violence could be eliminated, racism would turn out to be a relatively unimportant factor.

Look at the integration of Asian and white communities, in the West especially. Non-white Asians do not depress property values; their crime rates are probably lower than most native Americans. While some people may resent Chinese or Japanese or Filipinos moving into a neighborhood, it is not a source of great conflict or tension.

I don't want to deny the racism in a lot of neighborhoods, but it is a mistake to write off such social tensions as all being attributable to racism, because then you ignore some of the real social problems that exist.

Could you be a little more specific?

Harold Washington, the recently deceased mayor of Chicago, promised during his election to set up some kind of property value insurance for neighborhoods in the city, and then reneged on that after the election, which was most unfortunate. I can't imagine a more effective way of reducing racial tension in the city than through property value insurance.

As a matter of fact, by having property value insurance, you would probably not need it. Once the property values were insured, they wouldn't go down, and so it would not be necessary to collect the insurance.

Racism still persists, then?

I would have to say that there's a lot of neighborhood bigotry, racial bigotry, perhaps rooted in problems of the past. There's less than there used to be.

When I was at Christ the King, there were some real Irish bigots who didn't like blacks at all. Now, Christ the King is a peacefully, and, it looks, a stably integrated neighborhood. Many of the bigots' children are living there in tranquility, with their kids going to school with black kids.

Racism is diminishing, and I would agree with my colleagues like William Julius Wilson who say that the problem in American society is no longer a race, but a class problem. Poor whites, poor blacks and poor browns all suffer from the same handicaps—social handicaps, educational handicaps.

What about anti-Semitism?

There's a lot less of it in this country than in Europe. I am horrified every time I go to England and I hear anti-Semitic jokes. I am horrified by some of the European clergy, not excluding some of those in the Vatican who, it seems to me, are very insensitive about Jewish matters.

Sure, there is anti-Semitism in this country, but it has diminished tremendously. But if I was Jewish, I'd be nervous.

Are racism and anti-Semitism irrational things that are part of human nature? How do you explain them?

Humankind doesn't take easily to diversity. We are normally threatened by people who are different from us. Those of us who are emotionally handicapped are particularly likely to blame our problems on those that are different. Humans seem to need a scapegoat. People that are different, religiously or racially, make excellent scapegoats, unfortunately.

Another quote from Andrew Greeley: "Catholics tend to understand the neighborhoods better than anyone else." How so?

The Catholic imagination, David Tracy's analogical imagination, encourages us to see networks of relationships and to see these networks as reflections of God. So we don't see community as necessarily restraining. We see communities as mediators. And we don't view society as oppressive, but as necessary. We see people as social beings.

I don't think that's part of the Protestant imagination. Protestant imagination sees it as the individual over against God, and views intervening communities as really getting in the way of that relationship. Analogically in the Catholic imagination, there is a tilt towards community.

But Protestants form neighborhoods, don't they?

I don't think they form them as intensely as we do. The data show that they feel a lot easier about leaving neighborhoods than we do.

Are neighborhoods important to cities?

Oh, yes. They're what keep cities together. Otherwise you have things like the housing projects, where there is chaos, no social control. Neighborhoods help to organize the social structure in the city.

What are the important neighborhood institutions?

There is the church and the school, and the ward committee members, the alderman's office. There is the drugstore, the pool hall, the grocery store, the business section, the delicatessen, the convenience stores—all of which might be viewed as the neighborhood shopping mall. And, of course, the playground, which is often the parish schoolyard.

A lot of those activities are taking place in the suburban malls.

Or in mall-like places, which also become locales. For a teenager, "mall-crawling" is the thing to do. It's like hanging around in front of the drugstore.

VII
ETHNICITY

"Being successful in America has not required us to give up our heritage."

Andrew M. Greeley

Ireland

Are you an ethnic?

Oh, yes. I'm a white ethnic. One of the things that offends me is that the term "ethnic," which was brought back into wide use in our society in America to refer to white ethnics—that is to say, to the children, the grandchildren and the great-grandchildren of European immigrants—was taken away from us.

It now means black, Hispanic, Asian, Eskimo, Indian American and Somoan. Those are the ethnic groups the Census Bureau recognizes, and that is how ethnic is normally used in the press. So, I don't know what we are to call the descendants of the Irish, German, Italians and Polish, et cetera, et cetera, et cetera. It seems to me that that term is no longer ours. But I am a white ethnic.

What does that mean?

I am an Irish Catholic. It means that I am someone who is influenced by my ancestral heritage, and that I know that.

There are two kinds of white ethnics. There are those who realize that their Irish or Italian or Polish backgrounds influence them. And there are those who try to keep it to themselves. That's the difference.

How did you get started studying ethnic groups?

As I mentioned yesterday, I started it because I was astonished that the sociological community was not studying it, and that it was not on any major questionnaires. Now, apparently, the reason for this is that American sociology, in the years after World War II, was shaped largely by the school at Columbia.

The two giants of that department, men who had enormous influence over students, were Robert King Merton and Paul Lazersfeld. Both of them were Jewish, both of them completely alienated from their own traditions, their own heritage. Merton's real name wasn't Merton. I don't know what it was, but anybody who is Jewish and calls himself Robert King Merton is obviously trying to change something!

How did they exert their influence?

These two Jewish giants at Columbia felt that part of their mission was to sanitize their Jewish students coming from the Bronx and Brooklyn and the lower East Side from their ethnic heritage—to make them Americans instead of Jews. So, they simply ignored the ethnic factor in American life on moral grounds. They believed that it was wrong, that ethnicity was not only unimportant, but that it shouldn't be important.

That's why sociology, for at least twenty years after the war, completely ignored ethnicity, and one of the reasons why they're still uneasy about it. They think it's, somehow or other, immoral.

What did you do to change that?

I grew up in a city where I couldn't ignore it. I thought it was crazy to ignore it. So, that's what got me into the study of it. I wanted to prove that it was still an important factor in American life. We did prove it.

My colleagues at the center at NORC and the younger generation of scholars who have studied at NORC have pretty much established that it is an important variable. We've shown that to leave the ethnic question off a questionnaire is as ridiculous as leaving an age or a sex question off the questionnaire, or an education, or a region-of-the-country question. No, I don't think we've convinced everybody, but we've intellectually won the argument.

And that has been your main area of research since?

Ethnicity has never been my principal sociological concern. It's always been religion, though I still look at ethnicity and still study ethnic correlations.

If there was so much resistance to it, how were you able to do the research?

The Ford Foundation began to fund our research in ethnicity because they were persuaded that white ethnics were a problem in American society; that white ethnics were somehow alienated; that they tended to be superpatriots and racists; and that the peace movements and the civil rights movements were a terrible threat to these people.

Is there still resistance to ethnicity today?

Having an Irish or Italian or a Polish name is still an obstacle in certain parts of society. There are certain areas where white ethnics are handicapped. But by and large, Irish and Italians have done very, very well in this country, and their income, occupation and prestige is above, way above, average. So, both these things can be true: it can be true that a group is generally very successful, and, at the same time, that there are invisible no-Irish-, no-Italian-need-apply signs on some doorways.

So, discrimination has diminished against the Irish and the Italians and the Poles. Society is not completely open to them, but it's fairly open.

Is ethnicity something that's only found in neighborhoods?

Oh, no. No, no, no. Ethnic subcultures are especially likely to be transmitted in neighborhoods, but they are in no way limited to neighborhoods. You find ethnicity everyplace, including the workplace.

I used to say that the difference between Pete Rossi and some of the other directors we've had at NORC was that when Pete wanted to talk to somebody, he'd go to their office instead of calling them into his. That's a behavior that's ethnic and Catholic. You'd go see your colleagues instead of bringing them to your office.

Wherever you have people with these backgrounds, their behavior's going to reflect their background.

So, people bring their ethnic behavior to their white-collar jobs?

I'm sure they bring it to the White House, and possibly to the Supreme Court. Now that we're getting a third Catholic on the Supreme Court it will be interesting to see how it effects the protocols of the Court.

Doesn't all this diversity threaten America's common culture?

No, on the contrary, it enriches America's common culture.

That's a good WASP question. The premise behind it is that everybody in America ought to be like everyone else; that is to say they ought to be like the people who were here first. But, in fact, even at the time of the writing of the Constitution, the wise men who founded this country knew that that could not be the case, and that they had to leave as much room for diversity as they could. So, our society has always been premised on cultural diversity. It requires only a minimal commitment, and that is to the political system.

Arthur Mann of the University of Chicago points out that the early immigration laws didn't have a language requirement. The new immigrants weren't required to speak English. You didn't have to speak English to become an American citizen until the beginning of this century. You didn't have to repudiate anything of your past; you simply had to accept the political system. You had to pledge allegiance to the Constitution. That was all that was required to be an American. Everything else was a matter of personal freedom.

What does ethnicity do for the society?

In fact, the way the ethnic groups have emerged in this society, they are not a way of differentiating yourself over and against society so much as a way of easing yourself into the society. As I've said many times in my writings, the hyphen in ethnic-American is an equal sign, rather than the slash. It's a way of becoming American. There are the Mexicans, the Puerto Ricans, there are the new Asian immigrants. They become ethnic groups here because it's a way of carving out for oneself a place in the society.

The image of America that was very popular in my childhood was the "melting pot." You were never exactly satisfied with that image.

No, to put it mildly, because, first of all, I don't think it's true; secondly, I don't think it should be true. I would hate to lose the richness of diversity that the various heritages and traditions have brought to America. Within a quarter-mile of this apartment you can eat Indian, Thai, a couple of different kinds of Chinese, French, Italian—a wide variety of cuisines.

Now, you can say, "Cuisines aren't important." But they are a good indicator. This society revels in the diversity of the foods because it revels in diversity.

You offered an alternate image to the melting pot: It was a "mosaic with permeable boundaries?"

Yes. "Mosaic with permeable boundaries" is the sociologist in me speaking. The novelist and poet much prefers Virgil Elizondo's image of the stew pot. That's neat. Potatoes can be Irish!

But explain the image. How does it—

You throw all these different things in, and they remain distinct from one another, but they all absorb the molecules from one another, so everything is flavored by everything else.

Did you once use the image of salad, or something like that?

No. As soon as I heard stew pot, I said, "That's for me." Now, I am very careful about taking other people's images; I always cite the source. So, if I use Jack Shea's theological images, I identify them; and if I use Virgil's stew pot image, I always say it's Virgil's.

Every time I've heard you use it, I've heard you give Virgil credit.

I'm currently using Godfrey Deikman's image of heaven as being a honeymoon. And I'll always give Godfrey credit.

Heaven is a honeymoon?

Oh, it's a wonderful metaphor. Heaven is a celebration, a fascination, a commitment, a pleasure, a challenge.

And it fits in with your understanding of God?

Yes. That's right.

Back to ethnicity. How do you explain what you call in your writings "the ethnic miracle?"

There are two miracles. One is that in the space of a single generation, children of immigrants actually do better in this country economically than the children who were born here.

That's an astonishing thing. The reason for it, of course, is that the immigrants are the ambitious people in any society. They sometimes say, facetiously, in Ireland, "All the ambitious people emigrated." That's an exaggeration that may not be fair to the Irish, but one of the things immigration has always done in America is given us a plentiful supply of ambitious and energetic people.

So, that's the real America.

In what way is it a miracle?

It takes about twelve to fifteen years, maybe, for an immigrant to achieve comparable income with a native-born American of the same educational attainment. Twelve to fifteen years and you've caught up! You're no longer driving a taxi cab after twelve years, and you're at least making the same amount of money that somebody with your training who's a native American is making. That's an astonishing achievement.

You said there were two ethnic miracles.

The other ethnic miracle is the fact that the ethnics have been able to sustain much of their own traditions—most notably, their religion, but also a lot of their family styles. Being successful in America has not required us to give up our heritage. The Irish remain Catholic; they have a literary style of their own. They didn't have to give it up.

Take Germany, for example. In first grade this year, there are more Turks than there are Germans. You ponder that, and say, "What's going to happen to Germany? Are those Turks going to have to become German, and can they become German?" That's the problem that our pluralistic culture will never have to face because all we would require is that these Turks in our society accept the political principles of the society, and they can be as Turkish as they want. The Germans will never be able to carry that off.

How do the ethnic miracles happen? How do they, in twelve years, manage to accomplish what they accomplish?

There's a restaurant over in the Benton Harbor area that I go to often in the summer—an Italian restaurant called Pasquali's. Mr. Pasquali and Mrs. Pasquali came here in the middle sixties, immigrants from Naples who knew how to make pasta. Their daughter was married last week. She has a Ph.D. from the University of Michigan, and she married another Ph.D.

How do they do it?

They did it the old-fashioned way.

What kind of help did they get?

I don't think we do any favors for immigrants in our society—as a matter of fact, the opposite is the case. But we let them earn the fruits of their labor. If they work hard, they can make it. They may not be able to make it every place; there may be all kinds of obstacles. This young women with a Ph.D. still worked as a waitress in a restaurant. She did not feel that it was all beneath her. She was not embarrassed by being a waitress in the family pizzeria at all.

Which ethnic groups have made it in our society?

Jews, Italians, Greeks, Chinese, Irish. The Eastern Europeans are in the process of making it. They are about drawing even with the national average. The Welsh and English and Scottish immigrants who came in great numbers in the last half of the last century and the early parts of this century came generally as skilled laborers anyhow, but they've made it. They're kind of invisible because they're in the Anglo-Saxon category, and we feel the Anglo-Saxons all came before the revolution. But, in fact, John Lindsay, the former mayor of New York, who is looked on essentially as a WASP, was the son of an immigrant.

Are there any who are not successful?

There are two groups that worry me. One is the Hispanics. What's wrong there, I don't know. But they don't seem to have made it at the same rate as others.

The other group is the Scotch-Irish, who got dead-ended, I suppose you could say, in the backwaters of Appalachia. They are now some of the poorest people in the country. There are white welfare cultures up in the mountains of Tennessee and West Virginia which are as depressed as any black welfare culture. In a city like Chicago, the Appalachian immigrants are pretty impoverished people.

There's a wonderful book called *Stinking Creek*, which I may have mentioned before. It's about the Appalachian subculture. Written from the inside, it's by a man who has a Ph.D. It's a very important book because it's a sympathetic defense of the Appalachian subculture. It says that it might not be all that bad if the Appalachians go into the cities to work to make enough money to move back to the hollows, because the culture of the hollows is very old in this country, and may be worth preserving.

But it may be that those two kinds of immigrants, the Hispanic ones and the Appalachian folk, both have the economic handicap of having a place they can return to very easily—they can return to Mexico, to Puerto Rico, to the hills—and that may effect their achievement.

In 1974, you said that the upward-mobility system was working for the European American ethnics. Was it working for blacks?

The picture is confused. The income of college-educated blacks who are married in the big cities of this country is higher than their counterpart whites. So, there is an emerging black middle class. It's doing very well indeed. They may still be the victims of prejudice, but they're not the economic victims of discrimination. That's a major achievement in our society for which we should be very proud.

But we still have the hardcore, welfare poor blacks—the people in the housing projects, the unmarried mothers, the kids that have three or four children before they're twenty or twenty-one. That is a tremendous social problem.

So, there is prejudice in our society, and there's probably some discrimination. But I don't think discrimination is, anymore, the core of the racial problem. The problem is poverty, and what happens to people who are impoverished from the day they're born.

How do they struggle out of it?

The biggest single contribution of the Catholic church in America is to give these people an option, an alternative educational system. It's an amazingly generous thing the church has done, and I don't think the church appreciates or understands it yet. We're far too eager to close the inner-city schools.

Didn't you say somewhere in your earlier writings that income was more important than education in the upward mobility of the American ethnic?

Oh, sure, but income and education are highly correlated. I mean, the new groups, the groups that are struggling, will sacrifice high education for high income. If it's a question of the kid either going on to graduate school, becoming a Ph.D. and teaching at a university or of his taking over his father's cement business, the pressure is for him to go into the cement business. It's only after you've received a certain amount of income parity that you can afford educational success or social prestige.

In your study on alcoholism and ethnicity, what groups did you pick?

The first ones we looked at were the Irish, the English, the Swedish, the Italians and the Jewish. Then we went on to look at the Polish, the Slovenians, the Hispanic and the Asians.

What were you trying to do in the study?

What we were studying was alcohol use in socialization; how alcohol use in various subcultures was getting transmitted across generational lines.

Why did you pick those groups?

We picked them because there was already a literature on them. And the reason there was already a literature on the Italians, the Irish and the Jews was that the first alcohol study was at Yale in New Haven, Connecticut. When the Yale alcohol people went out to find folks to study, that's what they found.

Then we went to the next wave of people. We went to them because there were certain expectations. Slovenia, for example, has the worst alcohol problem in Europe. Poland has a tremendous alcohol problem. As a matter of fact, the Irish, who drink too much altogether, are by no means the worst drinkers in this country or in Europe. The Eastern Europeans have far more alcohol problems.

Even the Old Country Irish rank sixth out of the nine European Common Market countries in per capita consumption, behind the French and the Italians.

So, while I would be the last one, God knows, to deny that Irish-Americans have alcohol problems, the stereotype, which may be in part true, makes the Irish look like the worst drinkers. By no means are they that. It's the Slovenians that have the most serious troubles.

They do?

Oh, terrible trouble.

My father's friend was an Italian immigrant. He commented on one of his son's opening a bar that, "If he opens in a Jewish neighborhood, the kid is going to go bankrupt in a couple of years."

Jews, generally, tend to drink when they're out to dinner. That's not a stereotype, it's research data. Your normal, in the sense of typical, Jewish drink is consumed before dinner in a restaurant.

What were the results of your study on alcoholism and ethnicity?

Basically, the different patterns of alcohol consumption of the ethnic groups we looked at were the result of different traditions. The problem got passed on from grandparent to parent to children. There's no need to invoke genetics or family structure to explain it.

It is often said that the Irishman most likely to drink is somebody who comes from a very unloving family. While that seems to be the case, you don't have to invoke that as an explanation. It's merely that people follow the pattern of alcohol consumption that they learned in their families or in their communities, growing up. That explains alcohol use, even alcohol abuse.

You seem to be distinguishing alcohol abuse and alcoholism.

When we began the project, we discovered in the alcohol research literature that somebody that has a drink every night before dinner is considered a heavy drinker. That led Bill McCready, my colleague in the study, to remark, "Everybody we know is a heavy drinker."

I would distinguish between alcohol abuse—that is to say drinking too much—and being an addict. I would not try to talk about addiction. We had some problem drinkers, but we didn't have enough real addicts in our sample to say anything about that.

So, there's nothing you could say about the treatment of alcoholics on the basis of your data?

I would say, on the basis of data, that anybody who comes from a family where there's been a lot of alcoholism should not drink or should be very careful about drinking.

On a practical level, whether it's genetic, whether these addicts have a weak gene, or not is less important than whether they grew up in an environment where there's addiction. The subculture of addiction is transmitted very easily. The research, and particularly the therapy now, that's being done on adult children of alcoholics seems to me to be very, very revealing in this respect. If you grew up in a family where there was alcoholism, you probably ought to get into a therapy group.

Why?

A researcher who wrote a book on it says the big problem with the adult children of alcoholics is that they have a hard time discovering what is real because there's been so much falsification in their lives, so much covering up.

According to their death certificates, both my grandfathers died of chronic alcoholism, but they also both died in their early or middle forties. I suspect that in Chicago at the turn of the century, that was a label that was put on the death certificate of any Irish workman that died young, in lieu of any other more elaborate explanation of why he died.

But still, neither my father nor mother drank, and they were very much opposed to drinking. My father's brother, I believe, was an alcoholic, and a number of my mother's brothers had similar problems. So we are very, very cautious about drinking, even in this generation.

As far as alcoholism is concerned, there's absolutely none of it in my family.

Italians don't have the problem. They consume large amounts of wine at meals, but they use it as a food. People don't get addicted to food the way they get addicted to alcohol.

The Yale research says that the Jewish subculture approaches wine as something sacred. The Italians approach it as food, and the Irish as an aid to gregariousness. You'd want to nuance that, but still, it's a good summary of the three subcultures.

That's interesting.

There are probably Jewish and Italian alcoholics, but I've never heard of one or met one.

What about the ethnic stereotype, the hardhat? Are white ethnics hawks?

Hell no. That's one of the evil myths of the elite media, for which there is not and never has been any confirmation.

Back in the time of the Vietnam War, when the hardhat was considered to be a quintessential hawk, the statistical data showed that construction workers were the group most likely to oppose the Vietnam War. They opposed it because their kids were fighting in it, and their kids were getting wounded and killed over there. So, to say that the white ethnics supported it was an exercise in bigotry.

We had a doctoral student at NORC who did a dissertation on ethnic working class chauvinism and bigotry. She was very much a product of the sixties, and she approached the project with a sixties perspective: she was going to expose ethnic bigotry. She could find no trace of it—no difference between the factory workers she studied and other Americans. Being a good scholar, she changed her mind and wrote it up straight.

What about racism?

I published a number of articles with others on ethnic attitudes towards race. Again, compared to the American average, the Irish and the Italians are not more racist, they're less racist. The Irish are the most pro-integration of any gentile group in America. It's not one study; it's study after study after study after study that indicates that.

After a while, you give up. You feel you're never going to persuade the media folks and the opinion-makers of the truth of this. You may not even persuade the Irish!

Are they liberal or conservative?

Catholics fall on the liberal end. They're not as liberal as Jews; they're a lot more liberal than Protestants. They're still Democrats. They still vote Democratic in congressional elections and senatorial elections. Given half a chance and a candidate that's worth something, they'll vote Democratic in national elections.

Moreover, Catholics were about as likely to vote for Reagan as one would predict. So Reagan got a smaller proportion of the Catholic vote than he got of the Protestant vote.

What about WASPS? Do they form an ethnic group?

John Shelton Reed from North Carolina has written about the Southerner as an ethnic. I would be inclined to say that there are a number of different WASP ethnic groups.

Oh?

There are a number of different kinds of WASP ethnic groups, both as subcultures, which pass on behavior patterns, and also perhaps with increasing self-consciousness of their traditions over against the rest of society. The Appalachians would be one; Southerners might be another; Texans might be another; Northeasteners, New Englanders, New Yorkers, might be yet others.

Those are impressions. Other than John Reed's work on the Southern ethnic groups, all I have are impressions, which are maybe hypotheses to be explored.

What about education and ethnicity? Is there any correlation between ethnic-related behaviors and education?

We have never been able to find any correlation between ethnic-related behaviors and education.

So education doesn't effect it one way or the other?

No. A college-educated Irish lawyer is likely to have a lot more in common with Mayor Daley than with an Anglo-Saxon or Jewish college-educated lawyer working for the same law firms. So, the various styles survive nicely with education taken into account.

What kinds of jobs do ethnics seek out?

When one talks of averages and not of everybody, Jews still tend toward self-employment and stay away from large companies; the Irish still tend towards law and government jobs. Interestingly enough, even Irish Protestants often choose government jobs.

In the academic world, the Irish are likely to go into political science and history, and are not likely to go into psychology or biology. Their Protestant counterparts are especially likely to go into education, or into biology. So, there are even different subcultures of occupational choice.

What happens in an ethnically mixed marriage?

That's a very difficult question to answer because it's hard to get sample sizes large enough to be able to talk about it.

We do know—from looking at the annual UCLA study of college students which Alexander Astin does—that by and large people tend to identify with the father's ethnic group because it's the name they bear. That group which is most likely to identify with the mother's ethnic group are the Italians: if your mother's Italian and your father's Irish, there is a fair chance that you will identify as Italian.

Does ethnicity persist as a distinctive factor in American political life?

It sure does.

Anywhere in particular?

It persists in all the big cities. It's called a machine coalition or an organization coalition. Ethnic politics has always been the politics of coalition.

We're going through a type of ethnic politics here in Chicago during the transition after Harold Washington's death. Eugene Sawyer, a black alderman, is apparently going to be elected today by a coalition of blacks and whites. Moreover, Timothy Evans, who is the Jesse Jackson black reform candidate, is reported to have the support of the five white ethnic aldermen who are generally thought to be loyal to Richard M. Daley, the state's attorney. So, you've got all kinds of interesting cross-patterns of affiliation and coalition movements going on. It's all very, very Irish!

Would you say that the dominant influence in American big-city politics has been the Irish political style?

Yes. Very much so.

And does that still apply to new cities, or does it apply to old industrial cities?

It would not apply to Tucson, for example. I don't know about Los Angeles. The only cities I would speak of with confidence are the cities in the Northeast and the central parts of the country.

Is there an ethnic dimension to national politics?

There's probably not enough of an ethnic dimension to it. Michael Funchian, in a collection of essays called *The Chicago Irish*, wonders why the Chicago Irish, so good at local politics, have never really done well in state or national politics. We've had one Irish governor—Governor Dunn, during the time of the first World War. We have never had an Irish United States senator representing Illinois.

The reason for this, Funchian suggests, is that Chicago is an ethnic island in a downstate Protestant sea. The Irish have never been able to build themselves a statewide organization because there's so few of them outside of Cook, St. Claire and a couple of other counties.

There are some distinctive voter behaviors among the various ethnic groups, aren't there?

The Irish and the Polish are the most likely to be Democratic, and the Italians somewhat less so. While it is certainly not true in this city, I suspect in the East, particularly in places like Boston and Hartford, the Italians may have been driven to the Republican Party because there wasn't any room for them in the Irish-dominated Democratic Party.

The older Italian-Americans are Republicans, and the younger ones are Democratic?

There may have been no room for them. I mean, in some of those cities—it was never true here. The Irish never had it sewn up here, so they had to let everybody else in. There was always room for Italians, Poles and Germans. Here it was never an Irish preserve as it is in cities like Boston and Hartford and perhaps Philadelphia.

VIII
RELIGION

"It is precisely because we're creatures capable of
hope...that we have religion."

Joe Patronite/Western Images

Religion is—true or false—fast becoming irrelevant in America?

Is it becoming irrelevant?

True or false?

Oh, false. That's nonsense. Absolute nonsense.

You have reason to believe otherwise?

It's not true that religion is becoming irrelevant anywhere in the world. One of the reasons we lost Iran, if we lost it, was that the State Department people who staffed the embassy there could not believe the possibility of Islam being a serious social force in the modern world. They've gone through all of the elite graduate schools where people are taught that the modern world is becoming secularized, that religion didn't matter anymore. So, of course Islam didn't matter; Iran was becoming a modernized industrialized society. A revolt? From a religious fundamentalist? Impossible!

The proper question is not why secularization hasn't occurred here, as it clearly hasn't, but why it has occurred in Western Europe and virtually nowhere else in the world. If it's happened at all, it's only happened in Europe. It's not a phenomenon anywhere else.

You're saying it's a European phenomenon?

I don't see data that it's anywhere else in the world. Certainly not in the Islamic countries. Certainly not in South America.

Why has religion declined in Europe?

Why it's declined in Europe is an interesting question to speculate about.

First of all, I'm not sure that the decline is all that much. Some French sociologists, even before the Second World War, laid out a map of the parishes in France where Vincent De Paul and his boys worked back in the 1700s, and then a map of church practice in France today. They were almost one-to-one correlations.

Now, that leads me to believe that in the French countryside there have always been low levels of religion. So, you have continuity rather than change even there. France has not been a religious country in a very formal sense.

What about the rest of Europe?

There's pretty strong evidence of a decline in church attendance in Germany and in Holland. I also think it's true probably for the Scotch, who were a good deal more devout at the turn of the century than they are now.

Then again, in some places—Ireland and Poland most notably, and in northern Italy—religious devotion continues. I don't know that the Italians are any less religious. I remember walking into the cathedral in the city of Como in Italy on a Sunday night, and it was jammed with people, as many men as women.

What about the Americans?

In the research I've done, I couldn't find a single bit of data which supports secularization. This book I have coming out with Harvard Press, which I mentioned, shows straight lines across the page. Religious attitudes and behavior don't vary.

My colleague Mike Hout from the University of California at Berkeley and I are working on a paper now about the relationship between age and religious practice. We are convinced that the cohorts don't change much, and that religion relates to the life cycle more than it does to cohort.

Mike and a research assistant are looking at some data on membership in church organizations. He's observed that young people don't belong to church organizations; older people do.

But how many people belong to church organizations?

At whatever age, women are four times as likely as men to belong to religiously affiliated organizations.

Thirty-two percent of Americans, in addition to belonging to church, belong to some kind of religious organization—the Knights of Columbus, the Catholic Family Movement, whatever. America has the largest number, far and away, of church-related organizations. Nothing even comes close to the proportion of Americans belonging to church organizations.

Church contributions tell another interesting story. In 1960, Protestant Americans were giving 2.2 percent of their income to a church, and they still are. Catholic contributions have declined sharply. But that's not a secularization phenomenon, it's not a result of Catholics going to church less, it's a result of Catholics being angry with church leadership. Belief in life after death, attitudes towards the Scriptures, frequency of prayer—they're straight lines, meaning there's very little change in people's attitudes over the years.

You mean, nothing has changed?

The one decline—and this is interesting—is in belief in the literal interpretation of the Bible. That suggests that the fundamentalist revival hasn't occurred either.

There has, God knows, been a change in attitudes on premarital sex—if that's religion. But on ordinary religious matters—you name it, and there hasn't been a change.

What kind of change has there been on premarital sex?

Whereas it was disapproved by most Americans, it's now tolerated by most Americans.

Really?

Oh, yes. Catholics more likely than Protestants. The real sexual revolution is not in behavior, it's in the acceptability of the behavior. And there is an area where we blew it. The Catholic church lost its sexual credibility with the birth control encyclical. People figured if the church could be so uninformed on the subject of marital sex, it was not a reliable teacher on anything that had to do with sex.

Does the data show that Americans have mystical experiences? Would you ever write a book, America: A Nation of Mystics?

I wrote an article in the *New York Times Magazine* with that title. So, the answer is yes!

It seems to have gone up recently, but at least a third of Americans, and a third of Icelanders, and a third of the Swiss, and a third of the English, report some kind of mystical experiences. About 5 percent have them often in their lives. These experiences correlate strongly with psychological well-being, that is to say, with happiness.

What kind of experiences are they?

These are Jamesian experiences, experiences where time stands still, and one sees the convergence and unity of the world, and all those kinds of things.

Do they have something to do with old age or lack of education?

They don't correlate with age; they don't correlate with education. They correlate a little bit with ethnicity—the Irish, whether they're Catholic or Protestant, are more likely to report them.

A decade and a half ago, I wrote a monograph called the *The Sociology of the Paranormal: A Preliminary Reconnaissance.* I became convinced, as a result of the work that went on, that psychic and mystical experiences are part of ordinary life. Forty-two percent report contact with the dead; 65 percent report ESP or deja vu experiences; a quarter report clairvoyant experiences. Mystical experiences are widespread in our society.

So, here's something that's been part of the human condition pretty much as long as we know, and the social sciences and medical sciences ignore it.

What about near-death experiences?

Raymond Moody's early research on near-death experiences finally introduced those experiences into the consideration of American scholarship. Now, I don't know what the near-death experience is. I don't believe it proves life after death. The most it has proven is an interlude around death when some wonderful things happen.

On the other hand, I would agree with Carol Zalesky, in her book, *Other World Journeys,* that there are signs, there are hints, there are symbols. She writes that these are illuminations and, as such, can be illuminating for those that have them, and instructive for those who do not have them.

These American mystics that you talk about, are they regular people? Or would they be called romanticists, people who are out of touch with what's going on?

I suppose they're, in great part, pretty much like everybody else. Some of them are romantics; some of them are out-of-touch. The ones I've interviewed are the healthiest of people. Their psychological well-being shows that. Moreover, they also tend to be very creative people— creative, energetic, outgoing people. Mysticism is good for you. They're not weirdos.

You're saying the paranormal is normal?

Paranormal is normal, and ecstasy is good for you.

You wrote a book on ecstasy.

Yes. In addition to the research report, I did a book called *Ecstasy: A Way of Knowing* for the Thomas Moore Press, which was a popular book. It was a review of what we knew about ecstatic experiences, and a description of the research findings. It stayed in print for a long time. I still get requests for it.

What was your point about ecstasy as a way of knowing?

Ecstatic experiences are noetic, that is to say, they're knowing experiences.

Aren't they limit experiences?

You could subsume them under the more general heading of limit experiences. But by no means are all limit experiences ecstatic. You can watch a little kid toddle across a floor and smile, and that could be a limit experience, that could be a hint of the presence of grace, but it's not ecstasy, it's not an instance of God kind of blowing in your ear, or something of that sort.

Could you talk a little bit more about what a limit experience is?

A limit experience is an experience where you come in contact with something that or someone who provides for you a hint of the transcendent. Any thing, any experience that hints of the transcendent, hints at the presence of grace, is a limit experience because it hints at something that goes beyond the limits of ordinary life.

You started before giving us some concrete descriptions of limit experiences. Could you give a couple more?

The kind of things that can be limit experiences in ordinary life are reconciliation after a quarrel; meeting an old friend, say, in an airport; a smile on a kid's face; Christmas dinner; the lights of the city at night...

What do we experience in limit experiences?

God!

What we really experience directly is gratuity. A goodness that doesn't have to be there but is. As Karl Jaspers says we get a hint that we're in a protective envelope that embraces us. It's on the fringes of our consciousness that we sense that something or someone else is there.

In your book Religion: A Secular Theory, *you talk about an experience of "otherness."*

Yes. If there is a gift, then very likely there's a giver, an "other" who gives. That's how we come to the notion of God.

Humans experience grace. We experience surprise, wonder, and these gifts—the surprise, the wonder—don't seem right to be there by themselves. We sense someone or something has to be responsible for it. That's otherness, or the other, or eventually maybe the other with a capital "O". The transcendent.

You say something about the experience being "preconscious."

They're not unconscious, these experiences of wonder, of transcendence. They also are not logical. We may reflect on them logically, but they occur prerationally, precognitively, in the intuitive dimension of the self. That aspect of the personality has very many different names.

Leonard Kubie, in his book *The Neurotic Distortion of the Creative Process*, calls it the preconscious, or the creative imagination. Kubie describes it as something lurking between the unconscious and the conscious. Jacques Maritain calls it creative intuition or the agent intellect.

What it really is is the poetic self, the creative self. We know, each one of us, that we have a creative aspect of the self, and it's there that religious experiences begin, first of all.

Are these the same as experiences of grace?

Sociologically, when I speak of grace, I mean a renewal of hope. Any experience which renews my hope is grace. Theologically, I mean the self-communication of God.

You call these limit experiences the basis of religion.

Yes. It's where religion starts, I'm convinced. Religion results from the phenomenon of hope being renewed. We are creatures born with two incurable diseases: life, through which we die, and hope, which says that death isn't the end. It's precisely because we're creatures capable of hope, mortal creatures capable of hope, that we have religion.

Now, that's the origin of religion, but it doesn't stop with that experience, it starts there. Then you encode those experiences in your memory as pictures—symbols—which point to something beyond themselves. Then you share those experiences with others through stories. But even when you've told the stories, that isn't where religion ends. We're reflective creatures, and we have to develop a reflective perspective to organize things for us.

I'm not an anti-intellectual; I don't want to condemn any of these things. They are all important; they're all central. But the origins come experientially.

Let's talk about this correlation you made between experience, image or symbols, and story. We've talked about the experience. How does the experience become symbol?

A symbol is an image that points to something beyond itself.

The example that I often use is this one. I am walking down Michigan Avenue in daylight, feeling grimly depressed because it's December and because it's a long time until spring. Then I encounter a woman who's having a hard time getting on a bus because she's got a child in one arm and lots of Christmas packages in the other. So, I hold the kid while she gets on the bus, and she turns around and smiles at me. The door closes, and she says thank you as the bus pulls away.

Suddenly the grayness is gone, and you've got a technicolor world in Dolby sound. If I could sing, I would walk up Michigan Avenue singing. So that's a limit experience. That's grace. The woman is sacrament for me, and I have received grace through her.

I encode my memory of her smile in the hard disk of my brain that's labeled "symbols." So her smile, the smile of a young mother with her first-born kid in her arms, points to the motherly love of God, points to the incredibly fertile and the passionately tender love of God. So, whenever I want to think about God's love, I recall her smile.

And how does it become story?

Then, if I walk into the Escargot Restaurant for lunch with some of my friends, and they see I'm grinning, and they say, "What's the matter, did you kill a book reviewer or something?"

Then I say, "No, no, no, no, no. Today I met a Madonna." Instantly, they know what I mean.

I've shared that experience with them through a story. I don't give them a curriculum vitae. I don't say how tall she is; what kind of coat she is wearing; that she talks funny and is probably from some place in the East; or guess where she went to school, because they couldn't care less. They want to know what happened. So I tell a story.

The purpose of the story is to call forth from the memories of my audience parallel experiences in their lives, stories of their own, stories of Madonna smiles that they've seen. Having done that, I've told my story. Storytelling is imagination leaping to imagination.

It seems like you're also creating a community.

Now, you could add a fourth step in my matrix of experience, image or symbol and story, and that's community, storytelling community. I can tell this Madonna experience of mine to my friends at the restaurant because they have been all part of the culture in which there are the same symbols. They know what Madonna is. All their lives, they've seen the Madonna, so they know instantly what I mean.

What's more important in developing good religious behavioral attitudes, the catechism or good Bible stories?

Good stories—Bible stories or stories of the saints, or whatever stories, but definitely stories, I'm sure.

Mind you, I'm not saying we don't need catechisms; we do. But we have to realize that catechisms are codifications, and reflections on experience. If there's no experience there to codify or reflect upon, the catechisms are empty.

We talked about hope, but I don't think we defined it.

Let me give you an early-Greeley definition of hope: The conviction that God is not mad, or, if you are a Christian, the conviction that God's insanity is benign.

The conviction that God is not mad is a quote from Clifford Geertz. If the world is absurd, crazy, then whoever is responsible for it is crazy. Therefore, whoever is responsible for it has a plan and purpose. A Christian addition to that is that the purpose is benign.

One of my friends—a correspondent, a writer—says that she wonders sometimes whether God is like a timberwolf, passionately devouring destructive forces.

I said, "You know, it's a nice metaphor." Francis Thompson thought of it first and wrote about it in his poem, "Hound of Heaven."

I would not want to deny to God the passionate hunger of a timberwolf or the relentless pursuit of that which she seeks and that which she loves. So, I'll accept the timberwolf metaphor. I would even say it's a good metaphor.

But neither would I deny to God the power of knowing and loving tenderly that we humans have. If we have it, why wouldn't God have it? So, if you want to say that God is a knowing and loving tender timberwolf—timberwolves, by the way, are very tender with their mates—okay, I'll accept the metaphor.

One last question about hope. How is it—I don't know if this is the right word—validated? How do we know our hope is not hopeless?

It's self-validating. You can reflect on it and come up with rational, philosophical arguments to support it—and since we humans are rational and philosophizing creatures, we have to do that—but ultimately, the experience validates itself. If you've had a hopeful experience, you know that there are grounds for hope.

What about the demonic?

It's clear that many of the graceful things in our lives can turn demonic, destructive. Our hunger for food, for sex, friendship, for independence, for security, can turn inwardly on ourselves and destroy us, or can turn outwardly and destroy others. But there is more to the demonic than the self-destructive propensities of our human nature.

I do think there are wars in heaven between good and evil. I don't know whether you have to postulate a personified evil, like the devil, though it's a remarkably useful model. It subsumes a lot of the data. But that there are evil energies that work in our world, it seems to me to be utterly clear.

What evil energies?

The two greatest nations in Europe during the early 1940s were presided over by madmen, Hitler and Stalin. Those two madmen were responsible for the deaths of maybe 100 million people. The two great wars probably killed maybe 200 million people, more people than have been in the human race in its whole history from the beginning up until about 1700 or maybe 1800.

Those are terrible, terrible events. It seems to me that they go far, far beyond mere human malice. I don't know how you explain these evil energies. I'm at a loss to explain them, but they're there.

Does the existence of the demonic, or of evil, somehow cancel or invalidate religion?

Not quite. Not quite.

You say somewhere in your book, Religion: A Secular Theory, *that people, when they experience grace, experience the world as good, but mixed with the not-good.*

But still good.

But still good?

Yes.

Would you explain that?

I see the woman smile on Michigan Avenue, and that's a wonderful experience. That's good. But then I also know that I will die and the woman will die and, eventually, will her son die. That's not good.

But I also know that a smile like that has a certain amount of eternity about it, and that's still good. The hint of the transcendent in that smile is "the still good." So, the world is good and not good and yet still good.

And is that what carries us over these experiences of evil?

Yes, that's the nature of a hope experience. Good, but mixed with not-good, but still good. That's what hope is.

What do you think people are seeking in the New Age movement?

They're seeking religion. I tell my students in Arizona—and we do pay attention to this stuff in our class—I tell them not to mess with any of those things unless they're absolutely solid in their own religious heritage and their own religious choice because when those things become a surrogate for religion, they can become powerfully destructive.

But is it basically a manifestation of the religious experience?

Yes. Something to believe in. Something to belong to.

And why do you think there are so many Catholics in those movements?

I don't think there are all that many Catholics in them. But to the extent that there are some the reason is that the church has become so arid for them, now. It's become devoid of emotion. The Sunday sermons are no good; the liturgies are pedestrian; what they get in schools from their teachers is largely social activism, devoid of any purely religious content. So, they turn to New Age, or to the charismatic, or whatever, for hope-renewal experiences.

Did you notice the New Age movement is also a sacramental movement? Have you seen how popular crystals are becoming?

Yes.

I know friends who are wearing and carrying those things like little sacramentals.

We abandoned that whole dimension of our religion. We abandoned medals and statues and crucifixes and rosaries.

It's Greeley's First Law—when Catholics give something up, abandon something, other people discover it. Greeley's Second Law is that when we discover something, other people are abandoning it.

The Third Law is that the propensity of an institution to interfere in the affairs of other institutions and tell them how to run themselves is in inverse proportion to that institution's ability to solve its own problems. So, the bishops go around offering advice to the government on foreign policy and economics precisely at a time when nobody has listened to them about religion or sex.

The title of your book Religion: A Secular Theory—*that's a contradiction, isn't it?*

No, it is not. It is a contradiction if you have a dialectical imagination, and you have to say "either/or." But the Catholic imagination, the analogical imagination, says "both/and."

The secular and sacred are not opposed to one another. The sacred is experienced initially in secular life. It is the purpose of religion to interpret and to correlate the sacred as it's experienced in the secular life.

My sociological model of religion explicitly rejects any dichotomy between the secular and the sacred. The sacred takes place initially and primarily in ordinary life.

That's what your novels demonstrate.

Yes. This is what I try to do in the novels.

You know, it's story theology put to the real test. Your image is the story of your relationship with God. It's the basic theme of the story of your life. If we can get at that, at your story of your relationship with God, then we're going to know a lot more about you. What's nice is that it actually works in practice. I mean, you don't always get that from social science theories, but this one works.

To a very considerable extent, my decision to engage in storytelling was shaped by that sociological finding. The evidence, the empirical verification, of the theory was so strong that I said to myself, "We need Catholic fiction again, writers like Graham Greene or Evelyn Waugh or Francois Mauriac—those kinds of people wrote."

Now, I don't propose to compare myself with them. Greene deserves the Nobel Prize. He hasn't received it, but he deserves it. I don't put myself in that category. On the other hand, I also have a very different Catholic vision than they do. Any comparisons I make with people like that have to do with purpose, not content or style or skill. I always have to say that.

IX
JESUS

"Look at Jesus, and you get the best hint we have
of what God is like."

Lake Shore view in Chicago

Andrew M. Greeley

You've made a lot of good statements about Jesus, but the one that has the most impact on me is the simple one, "Jesus' life was the story of what God was like." What you're telling me is that if I want to know what God is like, I have to look at the way Jesus—

Yes, that's the whole thing: Jesus is the sacrament of God. The whole purpose of having Jesus was to give us a notion of what God was like. We encounter God in the objects and events and the persons of our lives. We encounter God in the spouse, the parent, the child, the friend. But we encounter God especially in Jesus.

Jesus discloses God to us. Jesus is the self-revelation, par excellence, the best self-communication of God.

Is that the same thing as saying Jesus is divine?

It's much more important than saying Jesus is divine, because saying Jesus is divine doesn't say anything about what God is like. But saying that Jesus is the self-disclosure of God, the self-revelation of God, is to say to you, "Look at Jesus, and you get the best hint we have of what God is like."

I'm not saying Jesus isn't divine. When you say Jesus is divine, you don't automatically, in that statement, say anything about what God is like. That statement is a test item for orthodoxy. Having said that and passed the test, you haven't said anything about what God is like.

Now, do they come to the same thing ultimately? Sure. But, in the way we've been taught, that the divinity of Jesus means the sacramentality of Jesus, is a point that has not often been made.

Could you explain that?

To say that Jesus is divine is to say that Jesus is a sacrament, that Jesus is the Word of God, the best hint, the best sign of what we have of God.

How would you characterize Jesus for our times? Man for others? Man of hope? Liberator? Revolutionary? Storyteller?

The liberator and revolutionary terms, while valid in themselves, have an almost idolatrous overtone because they tend to identify Jesus with a specific ideology, Marxism. I find that idolatrous, as identifying him with capitalism would be idolatrous. It identifies Jesus with the contingent, with the problematic, with the uncertain.

I tend to think of Jesus as a man of wonder and surprise, a man who is absolutely not able to be fit into specific categories. Once we try to put a label or a category on him, then we miss him.

Anybody that claims to have figured out what Jesus was, what he was about, already doesn't understand him. Jesus came to surprise, to disconcert, to challenge our conformity. Once we have him figured out, that which we have figured out isn't Jesus anymore.

What is the very fundamental simple message of the good news that Jesus proclaimed?

That God loves us; that life is stronger than death.

And how did he explain that? How did he get that message across to us?

He told us stories, and his life was a story. He asserted that because of God's love for him, God would validate that love by not permitting death to destroy him; and that that would happen for us too.

When theologians summarize Jesus' message, they use the technical phrase, "The kingdom of God is at hand." How do you understand that?

I take the kingdom of God as meaning God's love is present. God's powerful love is present among us. That would be a good way to put it.

Why was that so overwhelming a message in Jesus' day?

The message was overwhelming because of the man who delivered it and the stories he told of what heaven is like, what the power and love of God are like—the Good Samaritan, the Indulgent Father.

What was striking was not so much that he preached the presence of God's power and love, but his descriptions of what it was like. His claim to know what God was like—that's what was disconcerting. That's what got him into trouble.

You say that the parables of Jesus are comic, that they are comedies of grace. What do you mean by that?

I mean that the Indulgent Father is a pretty funny guy. You've got him sitting on the front porch waiting for the kid to come home, and when he finally sees him, he gets up and makes a fool of himself. He goes running down to meet this kid who is a no-good. It's a very silly father who runs down to embrace a kid that has done nothing at all with his life.

You're talking about the parable we usually call the Prodigal Son?

Yes. Or, look at the farmer. He's paying people for not working. That's really comic.

Or take the Good Samaritan. It's funny to see this guy who is an enemy stopping by the side of the road to fix up the battered guy. Then, the funniest thing of all is he said, "Okay, I'll pay his board, and I'll come back later. If it costs more, I'll pay that too." That's odd behavior. Odd behavior is what makes us laugh.

But what do those parables tell us about God?

What they tell us is that, by human standards, God's love is crazy. Take the parable of the Judge. The judge waves off the woman taken in adultery. She doesn't even ask for forgiveness, he says, "Go and sin no more." That is truly mad behavior, scandalous behavior. So scandalous that it got cut from a lot of the editions of the Scriptures.

What about the parable of the Laborers in the Vineyard? You called it the parable of the Crazy Farmer.

He pays guys who are not working. He pays loafers. Look, it's harvest time, and there's plenty of work for everybody, and these guys are still loafing around. But he feels sorry for their families, so he pays them a whole day's wages for not working.

That one in particular is often preached on as a model for labor and management relations. Now that's ridiculous. Jesus isn't talking about labor and management relations, he's talking about the Father, about God, and saying that that's the way God is. God's love is crazy.

It's crazy and we can't predict it. What's the point of the parable of the Pearl of Great Price?

There are two kinds of parables. One is the set of parables of assurances, like the ones we've talked are about where Jesus is assuring us of God's love.

The other set of parables, the parables of urgency, are the opposite side of the coin. They say that you should seize the opportunities of the moment. And that's what the guy does. You can see the fellow loafing around the marketplace and coming across a tray of costume jewelry. He looks through, and does a double take because here is something worth millions.

He doesn't have money right now with him to buy it, so he dashes off and trades in everything he has and rushes back and buys the pearl. If something is that important, that valuable, oh boy, do you jump on it.

What about the parable of the Ten Virgins? Does that fall in the same category?

All of those parables are parables of urgency. The parable of the Buried Treasure fits into that category. Jesus wants to stir us out of our dullness. He wants us to live lives of enthusiasm.

Are there any parables in which God is portrayed as a woman?

There is imagery—for example, in the seventh chapter of St. John where Jesus compares himself to a nursing mother. But in all the parables, the Godlike person has always got a strain of tenderness, of affection, of gentleness.

What did Jesus teach about the relationship between the love of God and the love of neighbor?

He taught they were continuous; that they are correlates of one another; that the love of neighbor is both a sacrament of God's love and a consequence of it.

Could you illustrate?

Let's look at married love. As husband and wife, in your moments of highest passion for one another you value your love for each other more and you get a hint of what God is like. When you realize, "The way we feel about each other, that's the way God feels about us," then you begin to understand how God is love. So, your love for each other illumines God's love for you.

But it doesn't end there. Understanding God's love a little better— then that love of his illumines your love for one another.

This is the essence of correlation: that you permit the two experiences to illumine one another. The love of anyone tells us about God's love. Then, God's love validates and requires love for the other, whoever the other might be—whether it be the spouse or the injured enemy encountered on the road to Jericho.

What's the real meaning of the beatitudes?

The beatitudes all have the same meaning. What they would come to is, "Happy are those who trust in God."

The beatitudes are not new commandments. They are not moral obligations which Jesus is imposing on people. Unfortunately, what we try to do is make the beatitudes our new set of commandments, a set of obligations, new things that Christians really have to do.

That's not what they are at all. What they are is a description of the kinds of life that begin to become possible if you really believe in God's love. So, the word "meek," for example, does not mean wimpy. Meek means people who have a certain style, and a class; who live confidentially because of God's love.

Let's take three novels on the beatitudes: Happy Are the Meek, Happy Are the Clean of Heart *and* Happy Are Those Who Thirst for Justice. *How are you translating that theology of the beatitudes into the novels? Could you give—*

The novels are about people who behave that way. Lisa Malone in *Happy Are the Clean of Heart* is someone who dedicates herself totally and completely to her career.

There are all kinds of people in *Happy Are Those Who Thirst for Justice.* They are really hungry to pursue that which they see as God's will for themselves. In *Happy Are the Meek,* the hero and the heroine and their children are of the same sort. They are people who are meek in the sense that because they have some confidence in God's trust, they can act bravely and decisively in the world.

These are not things I make up. This is what the Scripture scholars tell us these words really mean. I get these from the *Jerome Biblical Commentary*—no greater authority can you find.

What about the Jesus "Abba" experience? That's the term he used to address God. It's equivalent to our "Daddy"?

It's a claim that Jesus makes of an intimacy with God. Apparently, no one else in his era dared to claim it. I suppose it's the quintessential revelation of who Jesus thought he was—someone with an extraordinarily intimate relationship with God. Someone who really knew what God was like.

But does it also say something about his image, what he thought God was like? Does it tell us what he felt God was like?

It tells us that God is, among other things, a passionately loving, foolishly indulgent parent. Abba makes the same point as the Prodigal Son/Indulgent Father story.

What about the suggestion of patriarchy in that usage?

That is imposing on the story an ideological concern of a later age. Jesus certainly spoke more of God as a father than as a mother. But the father of whom he spoke was always an androgynous character; always a gentle, affectionate and loving person.

What about Jesus' relationship with women?

If you want to find out what Jesus thinks about women, look at his relationships with them, which were extraordinary for a man of his time and for a religious leader of his era.

Leonard Swidler uses Jesus' attitude toward women as an argument for the incarnation. And I would agree with that—that only somebody with a very special link to God in that era could treat women with so much respect, affection and dignity.

What was special about the way Jesus treated women?

He always addressed them as equals. He respected them; he was close to them; he treated them as friends. Holy men in the Near East don't do that. They don't get involved in respectful and affectionate relationships with women.

Can you give an example from Jesus' life?

I like particularly the Martha/Mary thing. Now, we know that there obviously was a tradition of the Martha/Mary/Jesus stories which existed before the Gospel of which we only have a rather limited number available in the Scriptures.

Martha and Mary and Lazarus had to be teenagers because they weren't married—young people in that era who weren't married would have had to be in their early/middle teens. If you look at it that way, then you understand why Martha and Mary are spatting with one another. They're fighting as teenaged siblings do: "Why isn't she doing any work around here?"

Then, you begin to realize that what you have here are young people, kids, who are special favorites of Jesus, whose parents are probably dead because you never hear of them.

Jesus may even be kind of a surrogate parent or big brother to them. Both the girls have a crush on him, as girls that age do have on attractive men. Jesus does not flee that crush. He deals with it, and he treats both of them with respect and affection. That is tremendously impressive, particularly in that era.

I had never thought of those people as teenagers.

Of course they weren't teenagers the way we have them now. But they were kids. They're kids who were becoming aware of sexual attraction, and they both fall in love with Jesus. Jesus was flattered, and he loved them back. But he handled it as a mature adult would.

You title your book on Jesus, The Jesus Myth. *That gives the impression that Jesus the symbol is more important than Jesus the historical person.*

I wouldn't make that distinction. Jesus the historical person is a symbol, or he is a sacrament. To say that Jesus is sacrament or symbol is really saying that Jesus, the historical person, is the self-revelation of God.

By the word "myth," I don't mean something that's false, I mean a story that tells us about something beyond itself, or a story of God. "The Jesus myth" is a way of saying that Jesus is a story of God.

Let me quote something from Andrew Greeley about why the message of Jesus is relevant today: "It's relevant precisely because it provides the underpinnings of convictions about the basic nature of reality, without which we will never be able to change the world." Do you still agree with that?

Yes. There is entirely too much going off half-cocked about social and political issues in the church without any foundation in religious convictions or experience. It is as though we've written off the religious aspects of our tradition because they're no longer relevant, and we are going to substitute for them social and political activism. Of course, that'll dry up and dry up very quickly if it's not rooted in some fundamental conviction about an experience of God.

But you're not saying that we should sit back and accept "our station in life," as we used to say?

Oh, no!

What is it in Jesus' message that motivates social action?

That we must strive to love as God loves; therefore, we must strive to love everyone as God loves everyone; and, therefore, insofar as we're able, to eliminate poverty and injustice from the human condition.

To love the neighbor the way God loves us, you've got to experience God's love. But it does not follow that one waits to experience God's love and then goes out and loves the neighbor. We have already experienced God's love, particularly through Jesus.

So, through the self-disclosure of God in Jesus, there comes an impulse to social action. But you can't divorce social action from that impulse, which is what I see happening in a lot of the Catholic theological developments of the day. Religion is short-circuited, and activism becomes not a consequence of religion, which it surely is, but a surrogate for it.

The expression, "option for the poor"—does that come directly from Jesus' message?

I find the expression offensive. I find it especially offensive when the bishops use it, because they continue to keep people in poverty with the salaries they pay.

The Catholic social tradition has much more wisely in the past emphasized the construction of community and the reconciling of groups. An "option for the poor" is fine so long as you mean that you're going to do everything you can to eliminate poverty.

If, however, it means that you're going to get yourself involved on one side in the class war—which is the origin of the term and how it's often interpreted by people—then it's a very un-Catholic approach, in addition to being hilarious when it comes from bishops.

Would you agree with those who say that Jesus' message has not changed the world much?

I don't know that the validity of a message can be measured by whether it's changed the world. There has been progress since the coming of Jesus. We are, despite the holocausts and the wars, we are more sensitive to human rights and indignities and injustices then we were once. As the French novelist, Georges Bernanos, once said, we may be the first Christians. We may be early Christians. Christianity may be at its beginning.

What is your favorite parable?

I like the Crazy Farmer best. It'd make a great film.

We ought to call a couple of Catholics in the filmmaking business and say "We'd like you, Robert Redford, or you, Martin Sheen, to do a half-hour film or a fifteen-minute film on the parable on the Prodigal Son, or on the Good Samaritan. A story, no preaching; do the story, and we'll pay for it." Maybe do four of those, four fifteen-minute parables. Then you could have folks do a discussion afterwards, a real discussion, not one that's rehearsed beforehand, one where a bunch of people say, "What's the story mean? What's it about?"

You wrote an article or two, which I, unfortunately, haven't read, about film. You feel film is sacrament?

Film is the sacramental art par excellence. It has the most immediate impact on people's imaginations. It may not have the most powerful long-run impact.

The sacramental power of the film occurred to me in a really special way when I saw the end of the Sally Field film, *Places in the Heart,* which, if you remember, is a communion service in a Baptist church in which the cup and the plate are distributed to both the living and the dead—both those who are still alive and those who died in the course of the film are brought into the church to receive the sacrament.

When it was over, I sat there staring at the screen for five minutes, saying to myself, "I can't believe they did it, and I can believe even less they got away with it," but they did it, and they got away with it. And they made the whole point in the film in this incredibly mystical conclusion.

That convinced me, again, because I had already sort of realized it, that film is a very, very important religious art form.

Why hasn't the church, which is often called the "patron of the arts," been more involved with filmmaking?

The disengagement of the church from film is a result of historical accidents. The people who started the filmmaking industry were by and large, religiously alienated Jews. They were insensitive to religion, unconcerned about it, and were not particularly interested in having religious themes in their films.

On the other hand, the church that reacted to the films in those days in this country was a church that was trying desperately to protect the faith and morals of immigrants. So its response to the film industry was its own private rating system, the Legion of Decency.

I don't know whether it was a necessary response or not, but it was not a constructive one.

What do you think of Catholic film criticism today?

Now the movie industry rates its own films, and we do have Catholic film critics of highly erratic quality appearing in Catholic magazines and newspapers. Your typical film reviewer in your Catholic journals isn't very good.

A Catholic reviewer working in the secular arena, like Roger Ebert working out of a Catholic perspective, has extraordinary impact. There are now lots of Catholics in the industry. The president of CBS films, which is going to make the movie of *Angel Fire*, is Catholic. But the church has nothing to say to these people. It is absent from their work completely.

What advice do you have to the church with regard to its role in filmmaking?

Somebody said to me when the archdiocese of Los Angeles was last vacant, "Who do you think the next archbishop of Los Angeles should be?"

I said, "The most important thing of all is that it be somebody sensitive to the religious potential of filmmaking because he's going to be archbishop of the filmmaking capital of the world."

People laugh when you say that because it would never occur to anyone that the archbishop from Los Angeles should be concerned about the religious implications of filmmaking. Heaven knows, it would be very low on the agenda of Archbishop Mahoney, the present holder of that position.

So I am dismayed that a church which presided over the fine and the lively arts, which is responsible for the oratorio and the opera and the morality plays—out of which came modern music, modern drama, modern art—is so divorced from this new form of the lively arts. We don't commission films, we don't support them, we don't pay any attention to them except to condemn, and we have damn little to say to our own people who are involved in that industry.

Let me ask you a question similar to the bad question that I started with. If Jesus were alive today, would he be in Hollywood directing or producing films?

116

My answer would be the same—that mixes cultures. But filmmaking is something that is certainly continuous with the telling of parables. If Jesus were alive today he would support, much better than the church presently does, the Catholics that are engaged in that work.

What about the Catholics that are engaged in that work?

They go to church. Perhaps not quite as often as academics, but they go to church. They tend to be married in church. They define themselves as Catholics, so they're not alienated in the sense they're not about to leave.

And there is little they get from their parish, from their clergy or from their institutional church which at all helps them in their work, or illuminates them, or shows them the enormous religious power of what they're doing.

What about Catholic directors and producers? What do you think about their work?

Scorcese and Coppola are certainly working out of Catholic imaginations. *Mean Streets*, for example, and *Godfather II* and some of Coppola's films about young people—those are very, very definitely and profoundly Catholic works.

I don't know whether Francis Coppola realizes this. I'm sure Scorcese does. The religious themes in *Mean Streets* were so explicit that there is no way that Martin Scorcese wouldn't know that what he was doing was religious. I would say the same of his buddy, Robert DeNiro. DeNiro realizes that the roles he's acting are often religious roles.

Do you have any further reflections on Jesus that you want to make?

Yes. We have to be wary of recruiting Jesus as a carrier of our cause— he is the liberationist, or he is the conservative, or he is the guy that probably wouldn't preach in a parish unless he had the cardinal's permission.

Once we've done that, once we've made Jesus one of us—somebody who comforts us without challenging us, somebody who validates us without making us question ourselves—once we've domesticated Jesus, then he's not Jesus anymore.

X
GOD

"A beautiful and passionate woman or man is a
wonderful metaphor for God."

Andrew M. Greeley

Facade of old St. Patrick's Church

Is God a woman?

To be theologically accurate—and I now quote Rosemary Reuther—God is both male and female, and neither male nor female. In God, those characteristics which we consider both womanly and manly, both maternal and paternal, are combined. But, that being the case, it is perfectly legitimate for us to imagine God either way and both ways.

Pope John Paul II said we must think of God as our powerful father, but even more as our loving mother. That echoes something that's a minor key in the Catholic tradition, but it's there. It's been there since Jesus described himself as a woman, a nursing mother, in the metaphor in the seventh chapter of Saint John.

In the Middle Ages, they were prodigal, reckless, in the use of images to describe God. God is a mother, a father, a brother, a sister, a friend, a knight, a lord, a king—all of these things.

All of the human relationships described by those words were taken to be metaphors of God. The Middle-Agers weren't hampered by any fears that metaphors would be taken literally because they lived in an era when the difference between metaphors and prose was clear to everybody. In hyper-literalist days like ours, people get terribly nervous with metaphors about God.

Is God really as sexy as Jessica Lange, as you so often say?

My standard response is that She better be more sexy.

That comment gives me all sorts of trouble. It offends pious ears. But it is a perfectly sound theological statement. Moreover, it's the kind of theological statement that has to be made repeatedly so we can purge out the dualism and the puritanism which so affected the Catholic upbringing of most of us.

But in what sense is it true?

All human beauty reflects God's beauty. Human beauty that involves passion reflects God's passion. So, a beautiful and passionate woman or man is a wonderful metaphor for God.

If you can't accept that, then you're not really Catholic because not to accept that is, in effect, not to accept incarnation. If you start drawing lines, and say, "All forms of beauty reflect God except beauty that's sexually attractive," then you're talking nonsense.

So, that even when Jessica Lange gets to be sixty, she can still be an image of God?

Maybe more so. Maybe more so for those who love her.

How can God be God if, as you say, "She is elusive, reckless, vulnerable, joyous, unpredictable, irrepressible, unremittingly loving"?

I don't know. That's the way God is. That's the way God describes Himself/Herself in the Jewish Scriptures. That's the way Jesus describes the Father in the parables.

That's not the way the tradition that I learned in school described Him.

Too bad for the tradition; it's wrong. It's not the real tradition. You have to allow for the changes in culture and vocabulary, but what I'm describing is rather like what St. John of the Cross or St. Teresa of Avila described in their love poetry about God.

You mean, I wasn't taught church tradition?

The trouble is that when people talk about the tradition, they mean exactly what you meant there—what they learned in school. The tradition is what was taught in Catholic schools and in Catholic sermons between 1920 and 1960, that's the tradition they're talking about. The broader, richer and deeper tradition escapes them completely. They're unaware of it.

Somebody remarked that the biggest source of division among Catholics through the years is whether they take history seriously enough. If you don't take history seriously, you think that Catholicism is, as I say, what was taught in the parochial schools between 1920 and 1960. Or you think that Catholicism is the social action teachings since 1965.

If you do take history seriously, you realize the tradition is richer, deeper, more complex and a lot more fascinating, but also a lot more disconcerting. To properly understand the complexity and the richness of Catholic tradition is a real stumbling block to those who like clear, simple answers.

How about an example?

For example, in the birth control issue, there can be no question that the teaching church has emphasized this issue very strongly since when? Since Jesus? Since the late Middle Ages? No, since 1936!

I don't want to say it taught anything different before that, but I do want to say that it was not something that was emphasized the way it's been emphasized in the last half-century.

In the nineteenth century, when France was busy trying to solve its population problem, brought on by the combination of coitus interruptus—that's when the male withdraws before ejaculating—and abortion, the French bishops repeatedly inquired to Rome what was to be done about coitus interruptus. Repeatedly, the Holy Office responded by saying, "Do not trouble the conscience of the faithful."

Pope Leo XIII in the late nineteenth century wrote a whole encyclical on Christian marriage which didn't mention birth control once. That was when coitus interruptus was being practiced probably by every married couple in France.

Indeed, the birth control condemnation was not in the first draft of Casti Connubui, the papal encyclical of 1936. It was put in later on as a result of some lobbying pressure. I believe it was a Jesuit who talked the Pope into putting it in.

I don't want to say that the church approved of birth control, and I don't want to say that the emphasis on it now is necessarily wrong. I simply want to say that the history is more complicated than church leadership now is prepared to admit.

That's interesting.

Here's another example. In the early Middle Ages in England, there were all kinds of questions about permitting remarriage after divorce. St. Augustine of Canterbury and Pope Gregory corresponded back and forth on the issue. They came up with about six or seven or eight cases, including when somebody was freed from slavery, when remarriage after divorce would be permitted.

Now, I'm not saying we should go back to that, but I am saying that those who argue enthusiastically, if simple-mindedly, that the church has never tolerated marriage after divorce, don't know what they're talking about. They simply are ignorant of history.

Getting back to God, is there any "He" left in your God?

Oh, sure. Blackie Ryan in my novels is rigorous about using "He" and "She" the same number of times, shifting back and forth in the same sentence. I do the same thing in my nonfiction. But the reason I use "She"—some people say I use it to offend those that don't like it—is because it needs to be emphasized.

How does that jibe with the way the ordinary Christian thinks about God?

The research data show that almost 40 percent of American Catholics picture God as more mother than father, or at least equally mother and father. That doesn't correlate with age; it doesn't correlate with sex. I don't think it's an image that's new or feminist. It's an image that's been out there all along, and nobody has paid any attention to it.

A woman friend of mine said that anybody who's been a mother or had a mother, but especially anybody who's been a mother and held a newborn life in her arms, knows that's how God has to feel about us. So, we have to emphasize that.

In your recent article on liturgy in America *magazine, you say that for some people, father or mother, the birth of a child is a mystical experience.*

Uhm-hum.

People don't often think of the birth of a child as having any special significance for the father.

I would say they've never been a father.

In the research that Bill McCready and I did on mystical experiences, we found that childbirth was one of the most frequent triggers—more frequently for women, but also frequently for men. They're proud of the new life, too. It's theirs also, and they love it. They have participated in its production. Not infrequently, it's a very, very powerful religious experience for them.

In the experience that we have of otherness, do we experience God as something separate from us, or something related to us, something attached to us?

Something that pervades us, I would say. Surely, God is the Other. He is not the same as us, but He is not completely different from us, either, because we are absorbed in God.

In the experience of Otherness, the hope-renewal experience—particularly when that experience reaches mystical intensity—there is a sense of oneness. One of the people that William James quotes says that, "Of the two realities, I was less sure of my own than of His."

So, it's very much like being absorbed by God, while not losing our identity completely.

Is your God so incarnational that there's no room left for transcendence?

Oh, I don't think so. But the Catholic genius is to emphasize the incarnational. We should emphasize it as much as we can.

The Catholic imagination is not afraid of incarnation. It is not afraid of an immanent God. If there is something which distinguishes the Catholic imagination sharply from the Protestant imagination and the Jewish imagination and the Islamic one, it is that we are not afraid of tainting God by identifying God too closely with the world.

Do we create God in our own image and likeness?

That's what Voltaire said. I would rephrase it and say that we create God in the images acquired from the experiences which renew our hope. God is, if you will, a nominalization, a verbalization, of the reality of Otherness we experience when our hope is renewed. So, it's not in our own image that we create God, but it's rather in our images of grace that we get our pictures of God.

How does family affect our picture of God?

I suppose at the most basic and elementary psychological level. If our family experiences are such to generate a modicum of trust in our lives, then we have trusting images of God. If our family experiences tend to destroy trust, then God becomes an ogre.

Of course, there is an element in the Catholic tradition which has always tried to make God an ogre—the great Irish monsignor in the sky with the thorn stick, or a hanging judge, or what have you.

One gets appalled when one thinks about the God that was often taught to us in school, and may even still be taught.

My sister said to me once, "Why are they afraid to tell us how Jesus pictured God?" She said, "I know why. Because they're afraid we might sin if we really believed that." She's right. We used the ogre God to compel virtue because we weren't sure that people would respond to the loving God—a very un-Catholic position.

How do we get into positions like that?

When religion—formal religion, church religion, ecclesiastical religion—gets divorced from its experiential bases, from its pneumatic bases, I suppose you might say, then it's a pretty arid and sterile religion.

You see, my argument is that the self-communication of God doesn't vary. God is out there dancing with people, communicating Herself all over the place. It is the function of the church, ecclesiastical institutions, to correlate these grace experiences of ordinary life with the overarching experiences of our tradition.

Now, if secularization seems to occur, and people are less interested in the experiences of the tradition—they see no need for correlation between the hope-renewal of their life, and the hope-renewal that founded their religious tradition—there are one of two reasons that can explain that. One is that God has diminished his self-communication to people in their secular lives. The other is that the correlating people, ministers of religion, are failing to exercise their proper role.

We can reasonably assume that God is not failing. So, if, and to the extent that, the secularization occurs, it isn't God's fault, it's our fault.

Your data show that warm images of God have a very positive effect on personality development.

Yes, people with those kinds of images are more likely to be in fulfilling marriages; they are more likely to pray; they're more likely to have religious experiences. The image you have of God is a strong predictor of a whole range of social attitudes.

What's the effect of a warm image of God on married people and their relationship?

In a woman, none. But if a male has a warm image of God, both he and his wife are more likely to say—notably more likely, overwhelmingly more likely—to say that their sexual fulfillment is excellent.

What characters in your novels are God, in one way or another?

The lover, whoever the lover may be, is always God. The basic metaphor of my fiction is human passion as a metaphor for divine passion; so, whoever the pursuing lover is, that's God.

Does the image of God—this is a little repetitious—but does our image of God have anything to do with our sexual attitudes?

Yes, the more loving, generous and gracious our image of God, the better lovers we are.

XI
MARY

"Mary represents the tender, affectionate, mothering aspect of God."

Ireland

Andrew M. Greeley

What do you mean by the "Mary myth?"

Mary's role in the Catholic tradition, quite simply, has always been to be a sacrament of the holiness of God. That's a sociological statement, not a theological statement. It's simply a sociological analysis of the use we've made of the Mary metaphor down through the centuries in art, music and poetry.

Is she God?

No. Mary represents the tender, affectionate, mothering aspect of God. She represents that not only in terms of sociological function, but also in terms of influence on people's lives. That is an ecumenical asset, not an ecumenical liability. The Marian doctrines may be an ecumenical liability, perhaps, but the image of Mary the mother of Jesus, the Madonna, representing the mother love of God, is an enormous ecumenical asset. She's the only mother goddess in the marketplace.

Promptly the heresy hunters say she's not a goddess. Of course she's not a goddess. She's a human person, but she's a human person who tells us a lot about God—about God as mother. When I say she's the only mother goddess, that's what I mean.

When you talk about Mary that way, isn't that something unique that you've discovered about Mary?

I don't know that I could make that kind of claim. I suppose it first occurred to me what I read in Mircea Eliade's books in what we used to call comparative religion. Eliade, who was a Roumanian Orthodox Christian, juxtaposed Mary with all the mother goddesses. He's not saying that Mary is nothing more than these other goddesses. That's absurd. Images all have their contents and the contents are very different. But the structure of the image is the same. God is giver of life. God is nurturer of life. God is a tender, affectionate and passionate mother.

Catholic Christianity, unlike all the other religions, has not been afraid to absorb that instinct. The mother love of God, that human fertility tells us something about God's life-giving power—that's what Mary represents.

You give the Mary symbol a great deal of significance.

Henry Adams says it's the most important symbol in 1500 years of Western history and we—our theologians, our preachers, our hierarchy—try to ignore it.

Mary's not an important figure for us. I was sensitized to the importance of the Mary image by my good friend Harvey Gallagher Cox of Harvard University, who became famous through his book *The Secular City*.

Harvey has got one of the best sets of cultural antennae in the country. He wrote on our Lady of Guadalupe; it was in his book on festival, *The Feast of Fools*. I figured if Harvey had discovered the Mother of Jesus, maybe I'd better rediscover her. So I started going through and reading all the poetry I could get my hands on and thinking about it.

While I was doing this I got a call from the *New York Times* to do an article on Mary. I said, "Mary who?" "Mary, the Mother of Jesus," they said. That was maybe the most important article I ever wrote. The Mary research I did for it really shaped my paradigm for religion.

Basically I think you have to say that Mary is the distinctive symbol of Catholic Christianity, the one that distinguishes us from the other Yahwistic traditions, the one that best summarizes our conviction that created reality is a sacrament of God.

Is Mary a symbol outside of the Catholic church? I know that you're saying she should be, but is she?

I was talking to my class in Tucson once about this. We had done the research on the image of God, Jesus and Mary. I was focusing on Catholics. One of the young women in the class, a certain Colleen McBride—so you can tell where she's from—raised her hand and said, "Okay, so we know that Mary has got a warmer image than God and a warmer image than Jesus among Catholics. What about Protestants?"

I said, "Colleen, there aren't any Protestants in the project."

She said, "Sure there are."

"No, there aren't."

She says, "Yes, there are. We gave questionnaires to the spouses of the respondents. Don't tell me all those Catholics are married to other Catholics."

So I thought about it and said, "Colleen, you flunk! I'm the full professor. I have the bright ideas in this class." So I went home and played some games with the computer and sure enough she was right!

The Protestant image of Mary, though not quite as vivid as that of the Catholics, was still very strong indeed. As some Protestant kids said in the class the next day when I reported this—and I told Colleen she'd get an A—they said, "We may not buy the doctrines, but we think the Mother of Jesus has to be one of the most impressive persons that ever lived." I thought that was a very interesting comment.

I'm curious. Were there any Jewish respondents?

There were four or five Jewish people in our survey. They didn't have a very high image of Mary, which I thought was pretty poor ethnic loyalty! Perhaps they didn't realize that she was a Jewish mother!

In Ed McKenna's opera based on my novel *The Magic Cup*, the Mother of Jesus has a walk-on role. She and Brigid, the slave girl who is really the magic princess, have a bit of a verbal argument. Brigid says, "I know who you are. I don't care. I don't believe in you." To which the Mother of Jesus responds, "My dear, I don't care whether you believe in me or not. I believe in you."

When people say, "Is this opera all about the Irish?" I say, "No, we have a token Jew in it."

Are you involved with the production of the opera?

No, not really. I wrote the libretto. I'm involved, to some extent, financially. I'm supporting it with encouragement. But no, I'm not directing. I am utterly incapable of judging the music. However, we've produced the second act, and the critics loved it.

And it's premiering in March '88?

Yes.

In Chicago?

In Chicago.

I want to give you some titles that we give to Mary. I'd like you to respond to them. Blessed Virgin, let's start with that.

I don't use it because I prefer simply "the Mother of Jesus." That is her biological role and it is that on which everything else is based.

I understand what Blessed Virgin means and I certainly value the importance of spiritual virginity, but that term has gotten so mixed up with things like decent prom dresses and singing "Mother Beloved" at the end of the prom dance and that kind of stuff, that I am less comfortable with it than I am with Mother of Jesus. But I certainly wouldn't deny its validity.

What about "Mother of God?"

Again, that's fine. My friend, the former Apostolic Delegate Jean Jadot, when he read the first draft of *The Mary Myth*, said, "You say all these wonderful things about Mary. You never say she's the Mother of God." So I put a footnote in to address myself to that.

Surely she's the Mother of God—the *theotokos* of the early councils of the church. But to explain that, you have to understand the theology of the communication of idioms. That may be theologically accurate, but it's devilishly difficult to explain to people.

What about "Madonna"?

That's wonderful. I love that because it says "My Lady." It also has come to mean the mother and child picture. So that's fine. It's the Mother of Jesus representing the life-giving, tender affection of God.

What about "Our Lady"?

Okay. That's Madonna translated. Madonna has better meter to it.

Does venerating the Virgin denigrate womanhood?

I suppose there are ways to venerate her that certainly would. But in principal it ought not to.

In too many statues in recent years, she doesn't have a woman's body. We tried to pretend that she's a sexual neuter. We tried to make her into the negative sex goddess. We tried to deny those things about her womanliness which are most mysterious and most troubling. That denigrates women, and that's an abuse of the Mary tradition.

What about the woman, Mary? What was she like?

My position is this: if you want to know what Mary is like, look at her son. You can judge what kind of a mother the woman was by the kind of son she's produced. So if you want to reconstruct her character and personality, you don't do it by putting together the few passages in the Scriptures which were written without that goal in mind at all. You do it by looking at her son. Then you have some real notion of what she was like.

I'm prepared to give her walk-on roles in my novels, but only that. I'm very, very reluctant to ever try to put Jesus in a story. She and he are far too complex and disconcerting characters to try to reduce to print. I should add, though, that my first published short story, "Ms. Carpenter," was a little daring in that regard.

Tell us about the story.

An archbishop is told that there's a certain Ms. Carpenter outside that wants to see him. He says, "Of what age is this Ms. Carpenter?" The secretary says, "About nineteen." So in bounces this young, dark-skinned woman. Enthusiastic and vivacious. The Mother of Jesus. Mary Carpenter. After they talk a few moments, he realizes who she is and says, "What do you want? Are you going to ask me to build another church?"

She says, "Oh, no. I'd never be in one of those churches. If people want to build churches, that's fine. But no, I don't build churches."

So she argues with him, haggles with him really, about what she *does* want.

Finally he says, "They don't say in the tradition that you're a tough bargainer." She says, "I'm Jewish, what do you expect?"

You won an award for that, didn't you?

Yes, from the Catholic Press Association.

Was that your first published short story?

Yes.

You were off to a good start.

They haven't given me an award since, but that's all right.

The church's doctrines about Mary—the Immaculate Conception, the Virginal Birth, the Assumption into Heaven—what do they say about Mary?

I'm not a theologian and I don't feel particularly qualified to go into discussing the detailed implications of them. They all say the same thing, though: that she was a very special person who had a very special role to play in history. That special role she played tells us an enormous amount about God. That's the bottom line of those doctrines. That's the raw Catholic instinct that's been encoded in those doctrinal propositions.

How come there is all this respect for Mary in the church? Hasn't there been a very negative attitude towards women in the history of the church?

I don't know that it's been any more negative than anybody else in the Western world. I would argue to the contrary. The Mary image has had an enormous impact on civilizing men. For example, in the church, even probably today, women, nuns, have more check-signing power than they do in any other institution. The church is certainly guilty of chauvinism. But on the other hand, it's given women more power than most other corporations.

The church may have relatively little respect for women, but it has a good deal more than the pagan world knew before the coming of Jesus and before the veneration of Mary.

The problem is that we don't take our instincts seriously enough. In a certain sense, we have compromised between the Catholic instinct about the quality of women on the one hand, and the cultural forces which have combined through the years to keep women in secondary roles.

Catholicism should not be the last religion to ordain women priests. It should have been the first.

You think it will be the last?

No, the Orthodox will do it after us.

Is there anything in the Bible to prevent the ordination of women?

To my mind, no. Elizabeth Fiorenza's analysis of the question— with which, as I understand it, most Scripture scholars agree—would suggest that there were women who did exercise ministerial roles in the Pauline church. And that while the words "priest," "bishop" and "deacon" don't mean quite the same things now as they meant then, they were used indiscriminately of men and women then.

Women seemed to have presided over the Eucharist. Moreover, there's some historical evidence that women have also presided over the Eucharist in other times and other places, though it looks like there's a lot of cover-up of this.

Prisca, one of Paul's woman disciples, pretty clearly was the head of the community in whatever city she lived. I believe that the co-educational monasteries in Ireland were sometimes presided over by women. These women assigned priests to their duties, to the parishes around the monastery, and sometimes, perhaps, even ordained them.

There is almost no reasonable historical doubt that the women deacons were considered, in their time, to be in sacred orders; that there was no distinction between deacons and deaconesses in the early Middle Ages.

Why this reluctance to proceed with the ordination of women?

The real reason is that it means sharing power with somebody, and people don't like to share power.

At the Bishops' Synod on the Laity recently, the very suggestion that the ordination of women as deacons should be explored to see if it were possible was ruled out of court. You couldn't even investigate that possibility!

Of course, if the possibility were investigated, overwhelming evidence would be found that they could be. Then, the Vatican would be faced either with permitting this, or saying the evidence is wrong. So, they won't even look at the evidence.

That kind of behavior suggests not doctrine, but power and politics. Women could be ordained deacons tomorrow on the basis of the historical evidence that they were deacons once before.

Understanding power and politics as you do, do you think that's something we'll see in our lifetimes?

I would be very surprised. It's certainly not going to happen during the present pontificate. Moreover, the opposition to it in the Third World countries is overwhelming.

So, again, if it were to happen, it would have to be one of these cases where it was left at the option of local hierarchies. I don't think the present Vatican is likely to change and ordain women, and I don't think it's willing to give that kind of local option.

Did we actually have a female Pope?

I don't think so. I doubt it. That's legend.

Does Mary have any meaning to the younger generation?

Our data shows she sure does. She still represents what she always did. Have I told you my story about Mary, Jesus and St. Peter?

I don't think so.

[Slips into West of Ireland brogue.] One day Jesus was walking through heaven. He got quite a bit upset because there were some folks in heaven that ought not to have been there at all. Most of them should have been in purgatory until the end of time and some of them would have been awful lucky to make it to purgatory.

So he goes out to the front gate and there's your man Simon Peter sitting there with his 386 computer, his printouts and his fishing rod.

Jesus says to him, he says, "Simon Peter, you've blown it again. I can never rely on you. You never do things right."

Simon Peter says, "What's wrong now, Boss? What have I done wrong this time?"

"Well," says Jesus, "You know there's a lot of people getting through this gate that ought not to. I was walking through the streets of heaven and there's some terrible characters there. Terrible, terrible people. Why are you letting them in?"

Peter says, "I didn't let those folks in at all."

"Well now," says Jesus, "If you didn't let them in and you're the keeper of the keys in the Kingdom of Heaven, how did they get in?"

"Ah," says Simon Peter, "I turn them down and you know what they do?"

"No, what what do they do?" "Sure, they go around to the back door and your mother lets them in."

That's not very good theology, but it's a great story. It shows what essentially is the role of the Mary image in the Catholic tradition.

Bernard of Clairvaux put the same thing somewhat more prosaically, I guess, when he said, "If you fear the Father, go to the Son. If you fear the Son, go to the Mother."

Do any of the devotions to Mary have any meaning for Catholics today? The rosary, for example?

Some people in my generation still carry the rosary, but we saccharined that one out.

The devotions have to be recaptured. The easiest thing to recapture is the May crowning. It is a wonderful ceremony. There are some parishes that even have them nowadays. My friend Tom Connolly out in Tucson has nighttime processions through the desert, which are wonderful.

What about your novels? Are any of your characters Mary-like?

Oh, yes. Oh, yes. Most especially, Noele Farrell, the teenager in *Lord of the Dance*. Blackie Ryan's mother, Kate Collins Ryan, is a Mary figure. She only appears briefly and indirectly. At least two of the sisters, Eileen, the lawyer and the judge, and Mary Kate, the psychiatrist, they're both Mary figures.

All of my women—perhaps not surprisingly—kind of reflect my images of Mary. After all, it was my writing the book about Mary that in part made me think about doing fiction.

XII
SEX

"The passionate attraction between humans reveals
what God is like."

Andrew M. Greeley

Sailboat

Moving ahead to sexuality and marriage.

Um-hum, I'm for both.

That's good to hear, but you're really kidding when you say sex is a sacrament?

No, I'm not kidding. I'm serious. Of course it's a sacrament. Saint Paul said it. Marriage is a great sacrament. Human passion is the reflection of divine passion, that's what I mean.

Sacrament is an interesting example of how you take a perfectly good word, theologize it, and then deprive it of all its meaning. Sacrament, symbol, mysterion—they all mean the same thing. They all mean "sign." A sacrament is a sign of grace.

In the most elementary sense of the word, a sacrament could be called a metaphor. It's a reality that points to a reality beyond itself. So sexual passion is sacramental in the sense that it points to a reality beyond itself, namely, divine passion.

This is precisely what Saint Paul meant when he said marriage is a great sacrament.

But when you're talking about sex are you talking about romantic sex or are you talking about sexual intercourse?

Sex is sex. It's sexual intercourse, it's romantic sex, it's the sexuality that's structured into our being. It's all of those things.

Needless to say, it can be potentially demonic. It can be terribly destructive. But when one talks about the sacramental aspect of any reality, one doesn't talk about its destructiveness. Fire is a sacrament. Water is essentially a sacrament, the first of the sacraments. But water can be terribly destructive—hurricanes, tornados, floods, tidal waves.

How does sacrament with a small "s" relate to sacrament with a big "S"?

In one sense, I'll leave that one to the theologians. But in another sense, it seems to me that a sacrament with a small "s" is something that occasions an experience of grace in secular life. It discloses God's presence in the secular world.

A sacrament with a large "S" is an ecclesiastical sign whose function, among others, is to relate sacraments with a small "s" with the overarching experiences of our heritage and our tradition. So sacraments with a large "S" are correlative rituals. They correlate ordinary life with our religious heritage.

Could you explain that using marriage as an example? The Sacrament of Marriage?

The Sacrament of Marriage relates the passion of God's permanent commitment to us and sexual love. In that relationship or correlation between the two realities, married men and women understand, first of all, what God's love is like. God's love is something like what they feel for one another. But they also see that their love often strives to imitate the generosity and durability of God's love.

So the two illumine one another. That's what a correlation is. It's two realities mutually illuminating one another.

St. Paul shows this whenever he talks about marriage as a great sacrament. He can't make up his mind which the focus is. He keeps leaping back and forth between Christ and the church, and husband and wife. That's the nature of theology and correlation. You keep moving back and forth from one reality to another.

That's an important idea. Can you use a sacrament of your choice and give us another example?

The one I like is the Sacrament of Reconciliation, because reconciliations are so much a part of daily life. We're always being reconciled with our family and our friends, our lovers, our parents and our children. Life can't go on unless we're prepared to reconcile often. Reconciliation is often a prelude to even deeper and richer love.

You see, when we forgive and are forgiven by someone we love, God acts, God's involved in that forgiveness. When I forgive someone for something they've done or they forgive me, we're both acting in God's name. We're not giving sacramental absolution, but we're communicating God's forgiveness to one another.

The Sacrament of Reconciliation, then, correlates all these little reconciliation experiences in our daily life, draws them together, re-collects them, if you will, and then relates them to the great reconciliation of our tradition, the reconciliation of the human race with God in the incarnation of Jesus.

Now that's perfectly indisputable theology. No one's going to deny it.

Then why isn't this correlative aspect of sacramental actions preached or taught?

Because what we're usually taught is completely aprioristic: that it's sacramental grace which imposes itself and shapes human behavior, which, of course, in our daily experiences doesn't happen.

142

The Mass, we are told, or the Eucharist creates community. Sometimes perhaps it does. But more often, it simply relates human love to divine love. The Mass stands for community and reconciliation and love and life in the world and in the kingdom of the Father.

I guess my position is clear enough. These are enormously rich ideas. We usually destroy them by ignoring one part of the correlation, the human experience or grace. The Spirit doesn't dance in church, She dances wherever She wants. We know that from the Scriptures. The Spirit goes anywhere.

What's the impact of good sexual relationships on our religious imagination?

In our study of young Catholics, the better the sexual relationship between men and women, the more often they prayed, and vice versa. We don't know which comes first, but certainly the two are related to one another. Sex and prayer are intimately related, as much as that might offend some puritans.

That doesn't necessarily mean that good married partners pray together. I can't say that on the basis of the data, but it's probably wise that they do.

I was told by one theologian, one of my teachers in fact, that he thought marriage became a sacrament when sex became unnecessary to the relationship.

What an idiot!

How important is sex to marriage?

If it wasn't for sex, we wouldn't have marriage.

You get told by bishops and theologians and pious folk that sex isn't everything in marriage. I'll agree to that. But it's a hell of a big part of marriage.

If we weren't designed male and female, if we weren't designed for sexual union, then we wouldn't have marriage. Marriage is a public validation, a celebration of the propensity of human nature for the male and the female of the species to stay together in passionate affection while they raise their children. So, if it wasn't for sex, there wouldn't be marriage.

Moreover, while sex by itself doesn't guarantee marital happiness, it sure helps. It's pretty hard, for most people anyway, to have a satisfying marital relationship over the long run unless the sexual dimension of it is good. In the presence of good sexual relationships, a lot of other problems are much more easily solved.

You seem to have a cyclical view of married life: it starts with the honeymoon, it descends, and then there's an ascent.

I picked that up pretty much from my sister, Mary G. Durkin. She and Dr. Joan Anzia wrote a book, *Marital Intimacy*, in which they have a four-fold paradigm for marriage: falling in love, settling down, bottoming out and beginning again. Of course, it's precisely in that interval between bottoming out and beginning again when sex acts as the rubber band that holds the male and the female together—which is clearly what the evolutionary process designed it to do.

Is it a continuous cycle?

Yes. We have some data. Surely in the first ten years of marriage there's the *Kramer vs. Kramer* effect. Two good years, five or six bad ones, and then a tremendous rebound toward the end of the first decade of the marriage. It's also pretty clear that the twenty-fifth anniversary is a bad, bad time for married people. If they can get through that twenty-fifth anniversary celebration, it's usually pure gravy after that.

What happened to the notion that a family should have as many children as possible?

Was that ever a notion?

Wasn't that a Catholic notion?

It was something that was taught by some priests and some nuns and some Catholic lay people, but it doesn't strike me as being very sound Catholicism.

I suppose an attitude like that made sense when a family would have to have 6.5 pregnancies to produce two adults. If you have 6.5 pregnancies now, you're going to produce 6.5 children. If people reproduced at that rate the world would be miles deep in human beings in a couple centuries. If you refuse to take that fact into account, it's crazy.

What's the historical picture on adult life you alluded to? What are the statistics?

As recently as the turn of the century among the affluent in Europe, life expectancy was about forty-five years. Now it's seventy-five. In Western Europe in the first part of the last century—Eastern and Southern Europe into the latter part of the last century — the average marriage would last twelve years before one or the other of the spouses would be dead.

In the archdiocese of Chicago when I was in the seminary, the average age of a priest at the time of death was thirty-five years. To be a priest forever was to be a priest for ten, twelve years.

Now, what shaped that in great part were the epidemics, the typhoid and cholera epidemics of the last century about which we've forgotten. All kinds of priests and nuns died very, very young. However, it is proof that to be a priest forever meant ten years.

When my mother went off to the hospital to produce Mary Jule, not exactly understanding—I was six—I said, "Is there any danger in this?" Or something like that.

She said, "No, no. Only about one out of every hundred mothers die."

She had it right on. That was an accurate statistical description of maternal mortality rate in the 1930s. The 1930s! Now it's one in 20,000, 30,000, and then only in the complete absence of prenatal care.

You wonder what the act of sexual love meant to people in those days when the risks of death to mother or child or both were so high, one out of six for most of human history. I guess the best you can say is it was a given that they took for granted as one of those risks that came with living.

Do you think the church's thinking on birth control and divorce comes out of that?

I'll say this: the official theologians of the church and to some considerable extent, the unofficial ones too, have not taken into account these demographic transitions. It doesn't compute for them. The meaning of it doesn't get through to them. But you can't dismiss it. This is an enormous change in the whole matrix of social reality. You've got to pay attention to it.

Are Catholics more sexually conservative than other groups?

Not any more.

They used to be?

They were never much more conservative, and now on things like premarital sex and homosexuality and divorce, they're less conservative than Protestants.

Has there been a sexual revolution in our lifetime?

I don't think so, in general. Whenever people say there's a sexual revolution, I ask, "Compared to what?"

There was certainly a revolution in the last ten to fifteen years in some kinds of homosexual behavior. There was an explosion of bathhouse gay lifestyles. That certainly seems to be different.

It may be that the availability of cheap and effective birth control devices has led to more premarital sex. What may be the case is that the middle class is more relaxed in their sexual mores than it was fifty, seventy-five years ago. But the middle class is much bigger than it used to be, and it's been invaded by the children and the grandchildren of the working class and the agricultural class whose sexual behavior was always more relaxed.

So on balance, this so-called sexual revolution is greatly exaggerated, and over, too.

Why do you think it's over?

AIDS.

AIDS?

Herpes, but then especially AIDS, scared the living daylights out people.

It's absurd to say that AIDS is a punishment. It's a biological phenomenon. It's a disease like all other diseases. It happens to be a sexually transmitted disease. In a time when there are high levels of promiscuity, then this disease is going to be transmitted. Not because God is punishing someone, but it's the kind of disease that gets transmitted especially quickly in situations of promiscuity.

Why is the church so hung up on sex?

I don't know. You would think the way the Vatican acts today, it's the only thing Jesus talked about. Of course, he didn't talk much about it at all.

I suppose the explanation is that it's the last relic of Platonism and the conviction that people's bodies are evil. It's not our conviction.

Christianity would reject that, but we emerged in a world where that notion was pervasive and we're still stuck with it.

You think St. Augustine was one of the principal shapers of that attitude towards sex?

Oh yes. There have always been two strains in the tradition. There's Augustine and company thinking that sexual intercourse for pleasure was sinful, and then there's the theology of the marriage rituals, which look, quite properly, on sex and human love as an image of divine love. These existed side by side.

Pope John Paul II's audience talks are a definitive rejection of Augustine on sex. Though John Paul does not push the conclusions in his talk as far as they might be pushed, because he hasn't paid enough attention to the human sciences.

What do the human sciences have to say about sex?

That which is unique and specific about human sexuality is not its procreative, but its bonding dimensions.

Our sexuality was selected through an evolutionary process, not to produce primates, but to bind the male and the female of the species together. All the human sciences now conclude that.

The church is apparently unaware of that conclusion and is certainly not prepared to address itself to it, either to refute it or to learn from it.

The church is very, very interested in stemming what people call sexual permissiveness, and here is what you suggest that the church should do: A warm religious imagination does not produce sexual permissiveness, but seems to be the church's strongest asset in resisting sexual promiscuity.

The young people who have the warmest religious imaginations are the most likely to say that premarital intercourse is not good. That's in the data.

What is the role of sex in your novels?

I'm endlessly astonished by the adjective ''steamy'' predicated of my novels. It's a smear word and it's not true. The serious literary critics that you've read don't think it's true. In fact, most people that have read the books don't think it's true. But that myth, ''Priest writing steamy novels about the sexual life of priests to make money,'' is very pervasive.

147

The sex in my novels is very mild. It's milder perhaps than the sex in the Song of Solomon. Seventy-five to eighty percent of my readers, according to research done on them, find it tasteful and delicate in the sense they don't find it offensive at all.

So I've got a bum rap on that and I'm angry at the people that have given me the bum rap.

The role that sex has in your novels is to convey the passion of God toward humans?

It's to suggest that the passion or the attraction between humans reveals what God is like and that God works often through human life.

Sometimes the sex in your novels is demonic.

Sure. That bothers some puritans on both the left and the right. They only want nondemonic sex. Change the nature of the human condition and the human species, you'll have that. But if you're going to write stories about the human condition, some of the sex is going to be demonic. Does that say anything about the graciousness of God? It's a statement on the mystery of evil. How can a good thing turn bad? I don't know. I no more attempt to answer that in my novels than anybody can answer it. The theme of the novels is that the demonic always loses in the end. But, sometimes the end is pretty vague.

I see no point in minimizing the demonic forces of the world. What some folks want in the curious alliance of left and right is that all love in my novels be good and gracious and faithful and kind. My protagonists, male and female alike, are always in the process of becoming better lovers, but that doesn't mean that they're ever perfect lovers or that their sexual passions are ever free from demonic influences.

You say somewhere that you refuse to take responsibility for the moral behavior of your characters.

If a priest in a story is corrupt, then somehow that's my fault and I'm approving of the corruption. If the priest is lazy or tyrannical, I'm approving of that. If a priest has sexual hang-ups, I'm approving of that.

But that's ridiculous. It's a demand that only good characters appear in the stories. Only saints. No imperfect characters, no sinners. No one in need of redemption. Only those who are so good they don't need redemption. That's a ridiculous demand to make on a novel. Stories wouldn't be written if the only ones you could write about were saints.

Sixty-five percent of my readers say they have better images of the priesthood because of my novels. Only 6 percent find my portrayals diminish their image of the priesthood. And the proportion of Protestants having better images of priests is 70 percent.

Some of the letters that I read from the people who have read your novels and loved them were absolutely incredible. Some had religious conversions as a result of reading them.

Thousands, judging by the letters.

Those have been a tremendous help to me, especially in the beginning when *The Cardinal Sins* appeared. It was selling like crazy and I was getting clobbered all over the place for it.

The reviewers were usually attacking me, but there was no sign that they had the foggiest notion of what the book was about. I began to wonder whether this was truly the case that all those people who were reading the book didn't have any idea what it was about. Then the mail began to pour in, ten, twelve, fifteen to one, favorable.

Then I realized that the ordinary readers did indeed understand what the book was about and the difficulties were in the minds of the critics and not in the book.

XIII
THEOLOGY
"It's really a search for grace."

Andrew M. Greeley

Chicago

Let's start with something that you've been working on very recently. What is "the theology of popular culture"?

Dan Herr of the Thomas More Association had been pressing me to do a special newsletter on popular culture for a couple of years. I developed in it religious reflections on various popular culture genres: mysteries, westerns, science fiction, fantasy, romance, rock music, TV series, Woody Allen—those sorts of things.

What is the basic idea?

It's a theology only in the broad sense of the word because I don't deem myself a professional theologian. It's really a search for grace. A search for God as God is disclosed explicitly or implicitly in these various works of popular culture.

The underlying premise from the literary and sociological viewpoint is from the Harvard writer, Northrup Frye, who calls popular culture the secular scriptures. He says that the literary genres of romance and comedy contain the myths to explain life, which parallel the myths to be found in the Sacred Scriptures. So he sees popular culture, romance and comedy especially, playing a role in human lives, an explanation-bestowing role, analogous to the role of the stories of the Scriptures.

I searched in these various genres for signs of grace. If we must search for grace in ordinary life, then one of the places we should search for it is in the popular culture.

Tell us about some of them. What about the western, for example?

The western is easy because the western is the classic battle between good and evil pretty clearly defined.

Of course the guys in the white hat represent Jesus and the apostles! The lonely rider, the Lone Ranger, those are Christ figures. Self-sacrificing men who devote their lives to the service of good. The paradigm there is real easy.

Rock music?

I've been working on some rock musicians, most notably Bruce Springsteen, and more recently Madonna, finding the hints of grace in their work, too.

It doesn't come as any surprise to teenagers to be told that Madonna's song, "Like a Virgin," is a plea that a woman always be treated as something new, exciting and wonderful. It's perfectly clear to teenagers. I don't think it's clear to the kinds of adults who persist in writing Madonna off as a slut.

What she stands for is obvious to the fifteen and sixteen-year-old Madonna enthusiasts. She stands for the mixture of innocence and seductiveness that every growing teenager knows works in her body and soul. Madonna says that these things can be combined and they're both good.

Of course, every young woman seeking some meaning in life and some meaning in the various energies that are coursing through her body is delighted that at least someone is saying that, because most of her religious teachers are not. They have no notion that that's a problem for her, and if they did, they would likely respond with lectures. Madonna doesn't lecture.

Bruce Springsteen?

Springsteen, to some extent, in his live three-album set arranges the songs in the form of a story of his life. But to a much greater extent in *Tunnel of Love*, Springsteen is becoming a religious and moral prophet. It may be the most powerful prophetic voice raised in the country today.

In *Tunnel of Love*, he doesn't use the words, but he comes pretty close to describing original sin—the good he wants to do and the evil he does, the failures of love and the unintentional hurts done to the one you love. He also gets into the possibility of regeneration in water and light. "God's holy light," he says a couple of times.

In *Tunnel of Love* there is a sermon in every single song.

How do you thing the preachers and theologians are going to react to that?

I don't think very many clergy persons are interested in it. If you're given over to supporting the Sandinistas or Marxist revolution in South America, if those are your paradigms, then studying Bruce Springsteen and Madonna will seem almost blasphemous.

To suggest that they are both cultural indicators and possibly cultural prophets sounds so crazy that folks don't even want to listen to the arguments. That's too bad. If my premise is right, that grace is everywhere, and that God is communicating Herself everywhere, popular culture becomes a very important theological place—a place to look for hints of grace.

Fantasy?

One of the interesting, interesting themes that emerges is in that genre, most of which consists in grail quest stories in which somebody is chosen for a mission. They have to go out and do something—something minor like saving the universe or something of the sort! The good deed is something which only the hero of the story can do, and if he doesn't do it, it's not going to be done.

Is that true to life?

It's quite true. There are some things that if we don't do them, they're not going to be done. There are some people that depend on us rather completely. We are their knight in shining armor. We are their grail quester, and on our behavior, if not their salvation, at least much of their happiness depends.

Television?

I had an article in the *New York Times* last year about Bill Cosby as an evangelist. Bill Cosby's program provides wonderful paradigms for family life and wonderful lessons.

You walk into the church and get into the sermon and ask, "How many of you saw 'The Cosby Show' and 'Family Ties'? What was it about?" All the kids know.

Then you ask, "What's the lesson of the story?"

One kid says, "The lesson is that you shouldn't get caught lying."

Then another says, "That's not right, Father. The lesson is, you shouldn't lie."

These are the morality tales of our time. Since we have given up telling morality tales, people are finding them elsewhere. They're finding them in popular culture.

What about shows like "Dynasty" and "Dallas"?

I do not write about "Dynasty" and "Dallas" in my book on popular culture. But there are a lot worse things in the world than that.

What do I have to say about those television programs? Everybody in the world watches them because they're good stories. They are compelling stories. They hold people's attention.

They cornered a woman in Ireland when Ronald Reagan was coming to stay at Ashford Castle. Some of the Irish intellectuals and a couple of their bishops were upset about this. So they asked this woman what she thought of Reagan coming and staying at the hotel right outside that town. She said, "Actually, I suppose it's all right if he wants to come, but I ought to tell you the truth, I'd sooner J. R. and Sue Ellen come."

There's a wise woman!

Woody Allen?

Woody Allen, along perhaps with Martin Scorcese, is the only explicitly theological filmmaker in the United States today. He addresses himself to the question of whether God exists and what it means.

In *Hannah and Her Sisters* he gives an answer which is the same as Blaise Pascal's—it's a good gamble; it's a safe bet. If you live as though God exists, you're going to have a happier life, anyhow. If you're wrong, nothing is lost.

Whereas, if God does exist and you live as though he doesn't exist, then you've made some real serious mistakes. Allen — Mickey, the Allen character in *Hannah*—says "It's not much, but it's all we have and maybe it's enough." That's reasonably good. Pascal's "Gamble" is reasonably good theology.

Allen keeps changing his mind, so more recently he said any film in which he prescribes hope is not valid. But that will be reversed again. Allen is one of those poor people who can't help himself. He can't help hoping even though half the time he's not sure he should trust his hope.

What about the drug culture—the American drug culture? That goes along with rock music and—

No. Bruce Springsteen has never used drugs in his life, and he rarely drinks. Madonna doesn't drink or use drugs.

Are you serious?

God knows there is some coincidence between rock music and drugs. But most kids—most kids up to forty—now are rock music fans, but most of them don't use drugs. In any case, Springsteen, who is maybe the most influential rock musician since Elvis, doesn't touch them.

He's an Italian ethnic kid from Asbury Park, New Jersey. Once you realize that that's Springsteen's background, then his social position, his religious position and his sort of quasi-patriotism all falls into line. He's an ethnic.

So is Madonna. She's a daughter of upper-middle class Italians from Michigan.

I find that another one of the major contributions you have made to Catholic self-understanding in this country has been to articulate persistently that there is such a thing as a Catholic social ethic.

That's strange, because of course there's been a Catholic social ethic for ages.

When I was in the seminary, and in my early years in the priesthood, everybody knew the Catholic social ethic. Now, it's almost as if I'm the only one left that knows it. And when I repeat it, I'm making this big contribution.

Somehow after 1965 and the appearance of the Berrigans and the coming of Fr. Bryan Hehir to the U.S. Catholic Conference, the notion that there was a Catholic social ethic vanished. You try to talk about it now and people don't listen.

Now they're into liberation—Jesus the revolutionary, Jesus the Marxist. There will come a time when we will begin to value our tradition again, but right now we're in an era where anything that happened before 1965 does not matter.

You started it already, but could you articulate a list of the elements of the Catholic social ethic.

I tried to summarize it around three principles of personalism, pluralism and subsidiarity.

The first principle of personalism says that social groups exist for the good of the person. Persons do not exist to serve society; society exists to serve the enrichment and development of the individual person, which, of course, neither communism nor capitalism is able to work out.

The second principle is pluralism. It means that a healthy society involves not the individual and the state, but all kinds of intervening groups, organic groups that are established in the patterns of ordinary human relationships. The dignity and the freedom and the enhancement of the individual person is best served when social conditions are such that these intervening and intermediate groups are given a chance to flourish. Neighborhoods, the parishes, the work groups, even the management groups, the neighborhood organizations—all of these, either institutional or natural networks, are essential to facilitate the dignity and the freedom of the individual.

The third principle is subsidiary, which links the first two. It says nothing should be done by a larger or higher group which can be done by a lesser or a smaller group. It's the principle of decentralization. I recast it as, "No bigger than necessary." E.F. Schumacher's way of saying it is: "Small is beautiful."

That's the core contribution of the Catholic social ethic, and it's absolutely unique and absolutely important and it's ours. But we'd sooner have Jesus marked as a revolutionary, or make Che Guevara or Daniel Ortega into saints.

What about socialism and centralized government?

When there's a centralized society, you break up the natural structures, give all power to a single party. It seems that Catholics who are socially concerned now are persuaded that's the only way you're going to improve society. The overwhelming evidence is that it never improves society. So, in the bishops' pastoral on the economy, the principle of subsidiarity is hardly mentioned, then only to justify government intervention. The notion of subsidiarity and of decentralization by making decision-making power as low as possible in institutions—the bishops and their staff seem unaware that principle exists.

Does that Catholic social ethic lend itself to an American Catholic theology?

Oh, I would think so. The two ethnic miracles, the survival of ethnic subcultures and the enormous success of the ethnic immigrants and their children and grandchildren in our society, are really very important phenomena. They have a lot to tell us about the nature of the human condition, and the way humans can move about the world, and the kind of society which makes it possible for those folks to move around the world to achieve. They're extraordinarily interesting phenomena. Theologians, particularly American theologians, ought to reflect on the meaning of these phenomena.

You seem to be suggesting a theology of pluralism.

If William James is correct—and he is—that the world is a blooming, budding pluralism, than the United States, for all its flaws and faults, has coped better with human pluralism than any other large society in the world.

Our Catholic social theorists today, men like Father Hehir and the crowd around him, seem to have contempt for America's achievements. The ethnic diversity of our country is as natural as breathing air, and so we don't notice it as anything worth reflecting on. That's a mistake. We should reflect on it.

Is there anyone doing the kind of theologizing you're suggesting?

Not to my knowledge.

Michael Buckley in his new book, about the beginning of philosophical atheism, thinks the reason for an awful lot of the problems the church has today is the fact our theologians have responded to the problems of the modern world, not with theology but philosophy. That they have, in their philosophy, completely overlooked the importance of religious experience.

The importance of religious experience in the lives of people, and in the emergence of religion, is something to which very few theologians have paid any attention. It's not on their agenda.

Wasn't there a "Theology in America" group that you were associated with?

Yes, there was one here in Chicago and it may still be in operation for all I know.

I haven't heard much about it.

I found the discussions pretty frustrating. So many of the theologians were locked into a Marxist perspective. I don't mean to say they were communists or even that they had read Karl Marx, but their orientation was towards class conflict.

What keeps them from reflecting on the realities of the Catholic social ethic?

They seem to have a contempt for their own people and for their people's experiences. There's a sort of reveling in prophetic denunciation of their own people, which the bishops do in the pastoral letter on the economy. Archbishop Weakland did that. In his reflections around the country he condemned the Catholic middle class.

Yet the Catholic middle class pays the bills, to begin with. Secondly, if you look at any studies of their attitudes, you'll find that they had arrived at the same conclusions that the bishops had on many issues, long before the bishops did. The Catholic middle class is not politically reactionary. There are no grounds for the denunciation of them.

What do you think about the sociological analysis in the bishops' pastoral?

It wouldn't get a passing grade in a college class. I suspect the same thing is true of their economic analysis and their policy recommendations.

Someone told Fr. Hehir that there was nothing in the pastoral about productivity, nothing about the importance of productivity. He said, "Yes, it's referred to in two paragraphs." But how you are going to improve the quality of your life without improving productivity is something that apparently had never occurred to him to ask.

What produced this turn of events?

Father Hehir and his cronies are essentially redistributionists. They believe in taking from the rich to give to the poor. It's fairly clear in modern economic research that there's an upper limit on how much of that can be effective.

The GINI ratios, which measure the ratio of the portion of income between the highest of the population and the lowest, are relatively invariant in the industrial world. It doesn't matter where you look at it, whether in capitalist, socialist or mixed economies, the distribution of incomes is pretty much the same.

The way you're going to improve the lot of the poor is to increase the size of the pie. Again, the bishops and their staffs don't seem to comprehend that. They really want to take money from the rich and give it to the poor. Although all the evidence is that higher tax rates lead to a decline in the status of the poor because they lead to a decline in economic production.

So, what do you think of the bishops as economic analysts?

In general, I don't think they know what they're talking about. And they really didn't listen to the experts. They listened to the experts their staffs wanted them to listen to, who generally had a very hard-core ideological bias.

The bishops are hypocrites because they don't practice what they preach. For the bishops to invoke the so-called fundamental option for the poor, and to do so publicly and with great self-congratulation when they pay poverty wages to their own help, particularly to the employees of Catholic schools, is a sin. Nobody's ever responded to that criticism. I keep saying that, and it keeps getting ignored.

This Catholic social ethic that you're talking about—is it specifically American or is it universal?

Oh no, it's universal.

Does it go far back in tradition?

In its origins, it certainly goes back to Aquinas. It's pretty hard to trace it from Aquinas. But exactly how it developed—there's monographic or dissertation work to be done there. It should be done at the American Catholic universities, but nobody's doing it.

How does it work out as an economic tool?

The monographic work has not been done to reflect on contemporary economic life from the perspective of the Catholic social ethic. It would favor, in general, a mixed economy with as much freedom as is compatible with the general welfare.

It would especially be skeptical of giantism, of mergers. Mergers never work. The airline industry is a marvelous example of what mergers do. It makes for greater inefficiency and less safety. Mergers look good on paper, but you don't treat people like bits of paper you can move around.

What about labor?

The Catholic social theory looks for a greater share by labor in management and the ownership of corporations. So our ethic would incline us to support employee stock ownership plans.

It inclines me to wish that the pilots could really buy United Airlines because they know more about running an airline, I would think, than anyone else.

Let me mention some theologies and get your reaction to them. Death of God theology?

Deader than a door nail.

Did it have any meaning?

I don't think it ever did in America.

What about liberation theology?

Marxist nonsense. Not good sociology, not good theology, probably not even good Marxism.

It's not good for the United States?

Utterly irrelevant to the United States.

What about the idea of base communities?

I remember, during one of the synods of bishops, we were at a daily press conference at which his Eminence, Cardinal Timothy Manning of Los Angeles, was presiding. Always a charming and an intelligent man, he was explaining to us the importance of the base communities to South American Catholics. Apparently he had learned from the black American delegation to the synod about these base communities.

So, I put up my hand and I said, "Eminence, do you think, when these folks talk about base communities, they have something in mind that might not be unlike our American neighborhood parishes?"

It stopped him dead in his tracks. He pondered, and he said, "Oh no, I don't think they mean that at all."

Maybe they didn't, but that's our counterpart, and they were there a long time before the base communities.

So, now we have our theologians and our thinkers and our folks who write for the *National Catholic Reporter* rushing around, heralding the base communities and apparently forgetting that the reason we don't have them is because we don't need them here. We have parishes.

Do you have any recommendations for American missionaries?

The American missionary? Yes, for American missionaries and theologians to try to impose liberation theology on the Third World is simply imperialism. To push Marxist social organizations is imperialism. Imperialism of the left, but that's no more appealing.

They should learn about the Catholic social ethic and promote that. In Latin America, especially, the church has never been able to get itself the hell out of politics. It was on the side of the right for centuries and now it's on the side of the left, but it's still involved with highly contingent political movements, always to its own discredit.

I don't think missionaries have any right to go to a country which is not their own and try to impose on the people of that country political ideas which the people really don't want. There's no evidence, despite what some would say, that the people in South America want Marxism. In the liberation of South American governments, time after time after time, the governments that have been purged have been social democracies, not Marxist ones.

That's interesting.

Yes. It's also a fact as plain as reading the front page of the *New York Times*, but it doesn't seem to have gotten through to the liberation theologians.

The theology of revolution?

I don't think that's any different from the theology of liberation. It links religion with highly contingent political powers. Sometimes it may be appropriate for theologians and clergy to be revolutionaries, but as a last resort, because revolutions kill. Revolutions mean violence and people get killed. Sometimes academics don't realize this.

But, to say that the teachings of Jesus underpin the revolutionary activists is to speak a lot of nonsense. You've got to really push those teachings to come to that conclusion. They do underpin social activism, social concern, but not that specific style of social concern.

A priest from the Philippines said, "You know, nothing could be worse than what we have now. So if the Marxists are going to make a change, then we've got to support the Marxists."

I said, "Hey, try Poland if you want to find something worse. Try any country where the Marxist government is in power."

Story theology?

That's very important, obviously. Certain conversations have had tremendous effect on me, particularly as it gets reflected through the work of David Tracy.

What about theologians like David Tracy and Jack Shea?

David is a great philosophical theologian. His theological paradigm of limit experience in the Catholic imagination has had an enormous influence on my sociological thinking and in my decisions as a storyteller.

Shea is not only a theologian who theologizes about storytelling, but actually tells stories that are theologically effective.

Do you have any idea where they picked up their ideas?

Shaggs—that's John Shea—picked them up on the streets. He's street people. His father's a cop. And David picked up his ideas from Bernard Lonergan, the Canadian theologian who taught in Rome for years. Some people find David hard to understand. I suppose if you are not willing to work at his books, they might be difficult. Unfortunately most clergy are not willing to work at theological understanding.

What do you think of Bernard Lonergan?

God be good to him, he was obviously one of the two or three greats in Catholic theology in this century.

Hans Kung?

Hans is a first-rate theologian who has suffered from misunderstanding and calumny. If you read the charges made against him by the Vatican, and his explanations, and the further charges and his further explanations, you see that they're distorting his position. Every time he tries to defend himself, they distort it even more.

Now, in his later years Hans was snappish with the Pope and the Vatican, which may not have been all that wise. I argued with him back in the late sixties that there was no point in taking the Vatican on in infallibility. That study of his on infallibility was a turning point which was simply unnecessary. He felt that it was necessary because he felt that infallibility was really what underpinned the church's ecumenical hard line.

I'm not convinced of that. But he's a fine creative thinker. His books on the church, on modern atheism and on belief in God are absolutely first-rate original theological creations. He's been a victim of enormous amounts of distortion, particularly in his own country and by his own friends in Catholicism.

Rosemary Reuther, the feminist theologian?

I've found most of her theological writings interesting.

Mary G. Durkin?

The woman's me sister!

She's been treated very unfairly because of that. She's been pushed around by a lot of hypocrites pretending to be feminists, and males pretending to be open-minded. I mention the chairman of the theology department of Notre Dame as one. Whether you want to leave it in the book or not is up to you, but I'll say it.

What contributions have Catholic schools made to the country?

Right now, the biggest contribution they make is providing an alternative educational system for inner-city minorities, which is the most impressive and the most generous thing the American church has ever done.

The research Jim Coleman and I have done has demonstrated pretty clearly that the Catholic schools are much better at it than the public schools. In fact, they're better at educating anyone, not only inner-city minorities. This inner-city minority ministry, which is often short-changed and treated shabbily by the church, is extremely important and really quite wonderful.

What have they done for Catholics?

They have produced, on the average, the best Catholics in America. In almost any measure you want to come up with, the people who have been to Catholic schools are better, even taking into account their family backgrounds.

Moreover, Catholic schools are great community builders. The most active and enthusiastic people in any parish are those who have their kids in schools, or those who have been to the schools.

They're also the most generous, financially, in terms of proportion of income, not raw dollars.

Aren't the schools a big financial burden?

When we did that study back in 1975 of Catholic schools, Bill McCready and I calculated that the schools pay for themselves in terms of the extra contributions from the people that went to them, and most especially, from the extra contributions of those who have kids in them.

We calculated that year that the budget of the Catholic schools was about $800 million. If you figure in tuition, and the surplus contributions of those with kids in the schools, that amounted to $800 million dollars. So, the Catholic schools paid for themselves.

I sometimes think that we wrote that finding in invisible ink, because nobody pays any attention to it. It's perfectly good data. Nobody has challenged the data, nobody has challenged the mathematics, they ignore it.

So, you think young yuppie Catholics are still going to be willing to send their children to Catholic schools and pay for it?

It depends on where the young yuppie Catholics are living. If she or he is living in the city, they are very likely to choose the Catholic schools because they are so much better than the public schools, and because they are a very inexpensive form of high-quality private education. So, they'll make that decision on rational economic grounds.

In the suburbs, if you build schools, people use them. Now, if you go for a decade or two without mentioning them and pretend you can do without them, and then you come along and announce, "Hey, we're going to have a school," that's another matter.

In the northwest side of Tucson, where I live and do parish work, there are no Catholic schools. Some people put their kids in buses and cars and send them across town to Catholic schools. All the Catholic schools that are in Tucson are filled. There are six or seven northwest side parishes in which the demand for Catholic schools is incredible. People want them.

Why do those people want Catholic schools?

I suspect it's for the same two reasons that our respondents in our first Catholic school study twenty-five years ago wanted them. First of all, because they think their kids will learn religion in them; secondly, because they think they're educationally superior.

Did your data show that Catholic schools make Catholics better Catholics?

That's another finding that has been ignored. A quarter of a century later, people talk as though we found the opposite.

Catholic educators are like priests. They've lost confidence in themselves and their work. Evidence to the contrary is simply tuned out. It's very sad.

What kind of Catholics do they produce?

They produce people who are closer to the church.

Where would the Catholics that they produce fall on the liberal/conservative spectrum?

In the '75 study we found that they were more likely to be liberal ecclesiastically because they were more likely to be in touch with church communication networks, and thus to understand what was going on and what the changes in the church meant.

On matters of race and anti-Semitism, they were also more liberal.

The Catholic schools don't work spectacularly, but no educational institution works spectacularly. But they do have an important effect.

Are Catholic schools divisive?

That was one of the cliches thrown at Catholic schools back in the late fifties and early sixties. We could find no evidence of that.

The people who went to them had lower scores on measures of racism and anti-Semitism. Moreover they were no more likely to have all Catholic friendship networks than those Catholics that went to public schools. So they are the very opposite of divisive.

What does the disappearance of the Catholic school mean for the future of Catholicism in this country?

It's the loss of a major positive socializing institution, one that made great contributions to the country and to Catholics.

"The religious orders of women are responsible for most of what is good in American Catholicism," according to Andrew Greeley.

They did so much more than we priests did—the schools, the hospitals. They worked harder and longer hours and got paid less. They had a lot more effect on the people. And now the religious orders are all disappearing, and that's sad.

Why do you think they're disappearing?

I don't know. I don't know. For all the goodness they did, there must have been something badly flawed in the structure, in the culture, in religious life—really badly flawed—that when the time to change came, they couldn't resist the disintegrating pressures.

The religious women I know, generally women in their late forties, early fifties, seem to live under very meaningful rules. The life-style required of them seems to be nonoppressive, and yet supportive. They seem to be, if anything, better women and more effective at what they do than their predecessors, but they're not getting any recruits. I don't know.

So, do you think there's a future to religious life?

Any human institution or organization that's responded to needs for 1500 years isn't going to vanish, but it's going to take a very different shape, and I don't know what that shape will be.

One possibility: something like the Irish monasteries in the past. You would have, in the same order, real anchorites, real monastics, people who live active lives under vows, single people who have active lives and have an affiliation with the community, and married people and their children who have an affiliation with the community. Cutting across each one of those, some people whose affiliations are permanent, and others whose affiliations are renewable.

XIV
CHURCH

"The parish is the church, but that is not the way chancery offices view it."

Andrew M. Greeley with his nieces Elizabeth (left) and Ann Durkin.

Is the Catholic church becoming more irrelevant?

Oh no, no. The Catholic church has not been in better shape at least since the thirteenth century when Thomas Aquinas, Francis of Assisi, Dominic and those folks were flitting around. No, the Catholic church is in great shape, in this country in any case. In terms of its tradition and heritage, it's never been stronger. There's been an only 1 percent increase in the exodus of Catholics from the church in the last quarter-century. Given the traumas we've gone through, that's astonishing.

The way the Catholic laity has survived and flourished in its faith and commitment in the twenty-five years of transition since the Vatican Council is almost miraculous. I would not have believed it possible beforehand. So the heritage, tradition, the lay folk, parochial communities are making it better.

What about the bishops?

The church as a community is in fine shape, but the church as an institution is really in terrible shape. And it's mostly because of the kinds of men that are made leaders. The institution's leadership is unspeakably sick. The Vatican wants people that are "safe"; that means people that are dull, uncreative and generally incompetent.

Are there any other problems?

Some of the problems are mind-boggling. The vocation thing—we desperately need more priests. You look out and you realize that the church leadership is paralyzed. If the Air Force was running short of jet pilots, they would stop at nothing to launch crash recruiting programs. They would recruit money, personnel, top-level programs and they would really work at it.

You know, in most Catholic dioceses one or two guys work at vocations—maybe a secretary, a part-time secretary, maybe a seminary rector or two helps—but that's not a crash program. Recruiting priests is not a high priority item on the agenda of any bishop that I know of. Certainly not in the Chicago archdiocese.

Anything else?

The second problem is money. The American Catholic Church has half the money available to us that we did a quarter of a century ago. Literally half! We get $6 billion in contributions a year, when we used to be getting as much as the Protestants, who collect $12 billion.

The leadership is paralyzed in the face of this reality. They don't pay any attention. They pretend it's not there. They try to deal with the problem by cutting back on budgets, by eliminating salary increases and that sort of thing.

What do you think of some of the press the Church has been getting lately—pedophilia among priests, for example?

Not good. That is a potentially explosive element in every diocese in the country. The bishops have been told that the lawsuits could total a billion dollars, and still essentially nothing is being done to cope with it.

One by one, as the cases become public, the media begin to go after the bishops. In one city they're suggesting that the bishop is a felon because of his failure to deal with the problem. I've said it in public so I don't hesitate to say it here: there's a potential disaster case in Chicago. The same paralysis that we seem to face when the questions are money or vocation rise with this issue.

Don't we have a few good bishops?

If you gave me time, I could think of a half dozen, but I don't want to embarrass them by mentioning them by name.

What would be your idea of an ideal bishop?

The ideal bishop, first of all, surrounds himself with the best minds he can find. Then, secondly, with the help of those best minds, he tries to create a consensus for dealing effectively and powerfully with the most acute problems. And thirdly, he tries to develop—and these are not necessarily in any order of importance—he tries to develop a vision for the future of the church toward the achievement of which he can rally his priests and lay people.

Why hasn't that happened?

Take the first one: usually bishops don't want the best minds: they much prefer mediocrity, because mediocrity doesn't threaten them. Mediocre people do what they're told, and they come cheap.

Would you apply the same criteria to the Pope, your ideal Pope?

When they had the papal election in '78, I wrote a job description called In Want of a Hopeful Holy Man Who Smiles. I guess that's still my job description for the Pope.

I have no question about John Paul II as either a holy man or a man who can smile, but I don't think he radiates the kind of hope that John Paul I or John XXIII did. That's a big loss for the church in the world. If you find no hope and joy in the papacy, then where the hell are you going to get it?

And so you think the current Pope is doing an okay job?

I didn't say that.

I read his earlier writings and he's one of the most gifted men that's ever been Pope. He's got an incredible array of talents. He was badly traumatized by the assassination attempt on his life.

But the big problem is that he sees the world—don't we all—from his own particular limited culture and perspective. That perspective is not helping him to understand the Western world.

That's a tragic mistake. Because if he could be more positive, more constructive and more hopeful and more willing to listen sensitively to what's happened in the Western world, he would go down as one of the great Popes of the world, given his enormous ability.

In some things he's very much misunderstood. He doesn't have any unnuanced thoughts. All his talks, for example, are classic examples of nuance.

What do you think of the men under him?

But if he is nuanced, some of the idiots surrounding him now are not, like the Red Baron, Cardinal Ratzinger. He's told homosexuals that they are objectively disordered. He's told Jews that they have to become Catholics. And he's told Americans that American capitalism is so materialist that spiritual values are impossible.

Those are expressions of Catholic teachings that are deliberately chosen to offend people. Somebody whose psychology is such that he has to go around saying things in the worse possible way to create the greatest possible offense, is not sufficiently mature emotionally to have the position that he has. I don't blame the Pope for what Ratzinger has said, save that the Pope gave him the job and he keeps him.

What about the Vatican Council? Was it a good news or a bad news?

Oh, it was good news. Failures to implement it skillfully had a terrible effect, resulting in a terrible waste. But still it's one of the greatest historical events in the history of the church. It's positive effects will be with us for centuries.

What about the birth control issue? You claim that it has been the occasion for a substantial decline in religious behavior which has occurred among Catholics since the early sixties.

A decline happened between '68 and '75 and then stopped. Michael Hout and I, in a recent article in *The American Sociological Review*, demonstrated again that that decline was indeed a birth control phenomenon.

When the encyclical came out, there were two predictions on how the laity would react. One was the Vatican expectation, that Catholics would—perhaps not enthusiastically—bow their heads in respectful obedience, do what the Pope said, and throw their birth control devices out of the medicine cabinet. The other was the cheerful prediction of the *Commonweal* crowd and other Catholic liberal enthusiasts that they would simply leave the church.

Both were wrong. Catholics kept whatever their method was in their medicine cabinets and they stayed with the church. They concluded that they were going to practice their Catholicism on their own terms.

The result then was neither a decline in birth control nor a decline in allegiance to the church. The result was the decline of the papal teaching authority.

So, in one of the crowning ironies of Catholic history, the very goal which led Paul VI to write the encyclical was countervened by the attempt to achieve it. He wrote to defend the teaching authority—he was afraid if he changed the birth control teaching, he would be hurting papal authority. In fact, the way he did not change did severe damage to papal authority.

What did the Pope overlook in his proclamation about birth control?

It might have been possible to reiterate the birth control prohibition in such a way as not to blow it, but the apodictic nature of that was a disaster. I'm not saying the Pope should have changed; I'm saying the style with which he refused to change was highly counterproductive. He listed all the reasons for change and then dismissed them. He didn't address them substantively—with the population explosion, for example. The teachings of Jesus—everybody knows that Jesus had nothing to say about contraception. It didn't occur to Jesus that that would be an issue. So, it's really the old Catholic natural law. That won't wash; it simply won't wash with people. Maybe it should, but it won't.

In fact, the human sciences suggest that what is specifically and uniquely human about sexuality in our species is its bonding dimensions. We humans are the most sexually preoccupied of any creature we know, and ready for sex at any time—precisely to bond the two partners together emotionally and psychologically so they can rear the children.

If human sexuality is precisely for bonding, then for husband and wife not to have sex, not to sleep together, which is finally what the Catholic teaching comes to, is unnatural.

Married lay people know that. They know that the purpose of sex in their marriage is to heal the wounds and the frictions of the common life. Without it, it would be very, very hard for a man and a woman to live in the same house together, much less in the same room.

But the church leadership does not seem to be able to comprehend this point. As a result, it's lost all credibility as far as sex, which gets us back to your question of premarital sex.

Among American Catholics, has this affected the church's authority on other issues besides sexual issues?

It's done two things that have affected authority. First of all, it has introduced a substantial trace of bitterness into the personalities of many Catholics. They indeed continue to receive the Sacraments and continue to limit the size of their families, but they're angry.

Secondly, in substantial part because of this anger and bitterness, they are skeptical of anything church leadership says, from the Pope on down to their pastor in their parish. They're really angry.

If they're angry, what keeps them loyal?

They can make a very important distinction between the clergy and the Catholic heritage. They're Catholic. They like being Catholic and they're not about to stop being Catholic. If your pastor or your bishop is a horse's ass, that's a shame, but it's not going to stop you from being Catholic.

You also attributed the church's irrelevance to the appointment of "the post-conciliar geek bishops."

After the Vatican Council the Vatican was scared stiff by the American bishops who they had thought before the Council had no ideas. It turned out that they had people like Cardinal Meyer and Bishop Ernie Primeau, all kinds of very articulate, very tough-minded, very independent people.

So, they proceeded to appoint and promote folks that were creeps. In the years right after the Council, we had a bunch of real meatheads made bishops and archbishops and cardinals. Folks who were out of touch with the reality of their people, out of touch with theology and sadly deficient in abilities, but safe.

Then in the Jean Jadot era, we began to get good bishops. After he left, they went back to promoting the geeks.

Now, may I ask about the one you called a crackpot?

Did I call him a crackpot?

Not Joe Bernardin. It was Cardinal Cody.

Did I call him a crackpot? No, I said he was a madcap tyrant. That was shorthand for sociopathic. He was a clinical sociopath. It's a shame, a tragedy. A tragedy for him and a tragedy for the people.

But the greater tragedy was that somebody who was that abnormal was made bishop of maybe the most important diocese in America, if not in the world, and kept in power for at least ten years after the Vatican knew it had made a terrible mistake.

How come the Vatican didn't know it made a terrible mistake when, from what I hear, in every diocese he'd been head of there were a series of complaints?

He got out usually ahead of the complaints, and he had lots of friends in the Vatican that covered for him. He paid them off.

What was the legacy he left Chicago?

A demoralized and atomized clergy. You know, what happened in the Cody era was that everybody hunkered down and did their own thing. The kind of networks of priests that existed in my day, which was an enormous help to me when I was ordained, simply doesn't exist anymore.

There's still enormous talent in this diocese, but it's all operated independently and on the fringes, and in fear of being found out.

What about the relationship between the chancery office and the parish?

The parish is the church, but that's not the way chancery offices view it. The chancery office's view is that the parish exists to serve them, instead of vice versa. All centralized bureaucracies work that way. It's not just the chancery office.

One of the big problems is that the bishops are easily intimidated by the crank mail they receive from the radical right.

But don't they know that that's happening, that that's where all of this writing is coming from?

The Romans want to believe these are the typical lay people because it suits their own proclivities and policies. It's surprising to me how many bishops think the letter-writers are typical. Even somebody as sophisticated as Archbishop Weakland of Milwaukee worries about the folks that write letters. It's ridiculous because the people that write complaints aren't typical. Those who have nothing to complain about don't write.

You were describing your concept of the function of the chancery office.

The chancery office ought to be a service center for the parish instead of the other way around. But for it to be that, it's going to need competent people who are capable of coming up with something that parishes need.

What happens now is that the typical chancery office generates programs—youth programs, evangelization programs—without any consultation with the parishes. Usually it sends out the materials and expects the parishes to do the things suggested, which, of course, by and large they don't. That stuff goes into the waste basket. For this the parish pays money! It supports this kind of mimeograph or Xerox administration.

What about the ministry of the laity? What do you have to say about that?

Pope John Paul says in his exhortations that in matters of sex and marriage, married lay people have a unique and indispensable contribution to make because of the charism of the Sacrament of matrimony. That's a position with which I agree.

He also says that public opinion surveys are not the only way to do this, to consult the laity. Again, I agree.

But the truth of the matter is that if the married laity have a unique and indispensable contribution to make, and the church itself understands they're not making it, it's because the institutions do not exist by which this contribution can be made.

One of the high agenda items would be evolving these institutions in consultation with the laity. They had lay people at the recent Bishop's Synod on the Laity, but they were hired lay people, people that worked for the church. By the fact that they worked with the church, they instantly became not bad, not unintelligent, but unrepresentative.

The laity also have a voice on many other issues. The Holy Spirit dances with the lay people. She can be heard speaking through the voices of the laity, and the church leadership is bound to listen to Her when She speaks in their voices.

What do you think the church, the institutional church, will look like in the next millennium?

Better, I hope! It will be less a renaissance monarchy. It will be more governed by the principle of subsidiarity. There will be more decentralization, more local authority. We will be returning to where we were before the invention of the steamship and the transatlantic cable.

How's that going to happen?

More awareness of the richness and the variety of its own traditions. More pluralism, more readiness to tolerate the person. It's going to happen through slow change and not without setbacks.

Minimally the Pope should retire at a certain age, and Popes should serve for limited terms. The history of the papacy is one of short terms. Long terms only began with Pope Pius IX, at the beginning of this century, and we've had almost nothing but long-term Popes since. I don't think that's good. It freezes the church in one style for too long.

I could see the same thing happening with bishops.

I'd like to see bishops elected, and elected for terms. I often make the comparison between my bishop and my mayor—John Cody and Richard Daley—of the fifties and the sixties and the seventies. One was the most competent municipal administrator in America, a man of extraordinary political ability, and the other one was crazy. We elected Daley; we didn't elect Cody.

Will we ever get an Italian Pope again?

I hope so. I would think that the Cardinal Archbishop of Milano might very be the next Pope.

Are you basing that prediction on your computer—did you put together a computer model?

Yes. It turned out to be good, too.

It turned out good?

Yes. It was right both times. It predicted—

John Paul the First?

Yes.

Could your computer model be used again to predict the next Pope?

Sure, it could. We would have to go through some effort to collect data on the electors. Again, that's something I might do if there's some advance indication that there's going to be a conflict.

XV
HIERARCHY

"With a few notable exceptions, the hierarchical leadership exists as a spectrum running from mediocre to psychopathic."

Andrew M. Greeley

Chicago

Let's start with the Pope—the present Pope. Do you think he has brought a particular ethnic style into his papacy?

No, I don't think so. His is a garrison style. He is a man who spent all his life in a church under siege, and he has brought that kind of style into the papacy. But I wouldn't say it's a Polish style—certainly not Polish-American, but also not Polish-Polish.

The Pope is a professor of philosophy. He's an Eastern European romantic intellectual. He has that style and that's not a bad style, but alas, in his particular case, it's perhaps inevitably mixed with the garrison mentality.

What does that mean?

It's the fear that if you don't straighten out the disorder in the church, the church is going to collapse in the face of its enemies.

I don't think that's the situation and I don't think it expresses enough faith in the Holy Spirit's ability to make do. Indeed, the Holy Spirit rather prefers chaos because there's more room for Her to "blow whether she will" in chaotic than in highly structured situations.

You appreciate highly his sexual ethics and the things that he has to say about sexuality?

Yes, what he did in the audience talks was a great historic turning point for Catholicism.

My sister, Mary G. Durkin, has written a book—*Feast of Love*—on that, so I would defer to her, but the tragedy is that most people don't know the audience talks, and most theologians aren't prepared to reflect seriously on them, which they ought to do.

Of course the conclusion, which reaffirms the birth control teaching, diminishes his message.

What, particularly, about sexuality did he say that you liked?

Most important is that he insists on the sacramentality of sex, on its disclosure of God's love.

I'll never forget the English edition of *L'Osservatore Romano*, the official Vatican newspaper, in which the headline said, "Pope Extols Spirituality of Nakedness." I don't know what the original Italian said, but I'm sure that somehow was a slip. He did indeed talk about naked human bodies and their impact on one another. I gather that that section of the audience talks really shook up some of the members of the Vatican.

My sister's book ought to be a major theological resource, but people don't read it. There's so much anger at the Pope among priests and among lay people that they are not prepared to admit the possibility that he might have said and done some very good things.

What's the anger about?

It's the perception that he's trying to undo the freedom that the Vatican Council created. I'm not sure that that's giving him a fair shake. The problem's a good deal more complicated. But that's certainly the impression that people are getting.

But then that's certainly the image that has been projected even in his most recent visit to this country. He projected at least the image of simply not listening to what people were saying. He sat there, and permitted intelligent speakers to say what they wanted to say, then he gave a response that did not indicate that he heard them.

This was true of the priests and bishops and lay people. His response to Donna Hanson, the lay woman who addressed him in San Francisco on television, looked like real rudeness, like male chauvinist rudeness. Now I don't think that's what was intended, but I've got to say that's what it looked like and that's how a lot of people reacted.

Do you think the Pope understands the American Catholic church?

No. But unfortunately he thinks he does. So do all the people in the Vatican. They think that they've got it all figured out, and they'll talk to you at great length about it.

They talk about materialism, consumerism, secularism, the loss of faith, selfishness and all that sort of stuff. They're off-the-wall wrong. They don't know what they're talking about. God knows there are problems in American culture. The American Catholic church—there are all kinds of things wrong with it, but those guys don't know what they are.

Is that where the Pope is getting his advice about the American Catholic church?

I don't think he needs their advice because that's his vision of things, too. He's been here so he thinks he knows what it's about. Surely the people around him, who probably draft some of his speeches about America, are no better informed than he is, even if they're Americans.

When the Pope was here he denounced the export of American culture, by which I suppose he means "Dynasty" and "Dallas." Those in the Vatican seem satisfied with this paradigm of Russia as godless atheism and the United States as godless consumerism. And they believe that the former is only a little bit worse than the latter. That is a deceptive and dangerous paradigm.

Has the church always thought the Pope to be infallible?

I'm not competent to make any statement in terms of history. There's always been an instinct that the gates of hell would not prevail against the rock of Peter. But there's been the parallel instinct which says that Popes are human and make mistakes.

The compromise, which emerged from Vatican Council I, is that the Pope is infallible in certain very, very rare sets of circumstances. These circumstances have perhaps only existed twice since Vatican Council I, and only once before it—in the case of the Immaculate Conception.

In the Vatican, there's a tendency to extend the notion of infallibility to every word the Pope says. In fact, of course, he's only infallible when he speaks *ex officio* on matters of faith and morals. So, that's a fairly narrow definition.

Is there a broader issue involved?

There's a wonderful book by Father Dione on the papacy and on the magisterium of the church.

His thesis is that whenever the extraordinary magisterium is exercised—the Immaculate Conception, basically—it's always done so in a most collegial fashion. The Pope surveys all the bishops in the world, they discuss, they write and they agonize.

Dione argues that if Protestant, Orthodox and Anglican scholars would look at the praxis of the infallible, extraordinary magisterium, they would find it not in the least objectionable.

But then he says the praxis of the ordinary magisterium—the everyday teaching authority of the church—is almost never collegial. He raises the question of whether that is a good idea. He asked whether it ought not to be possible to exercise the ordinary magisterium in the same way you do the extraordinary.

He says that to argue that the ordinary magisterium is infallible, too, once what a Pope teaches has been accepted by bishops around the world is, on the face of it, wrong. In the Vatican Council, five or six things which the ordinary magisterium had held to rigorously and condemned people for were nonetheless changed; these had to do with aspects of religious freedom, church and state, inspiration, revelation, the nature of the church, the mystical body of Christ, salvation outside the church.

So the ordinary magisterium can be changed. He goes on to say it is often changed and changed precisely because there have been people who've been brave enough to dissent.

You could conclude from his argument that dissent in some cases is a necessity for the church. The possibility of dissent is a necessity for the church in order that it might be able to grow and understand itself. That's what Dione seems to be suggesting.

Because of the complexity of the question, I'm not clear myself, but I don't think the issue is settled as to how far one may go and still be an obedient Catholic.

What about the Pope's encyclicals? Would you find any of them distinctive?

I would find good things in all of them. The ones on social justice are very important, though I don't think he comes down hard enough on subsidiarity as he might, given the centralizing tendencies in the world. Again, the problem is with the encyclicals as with so much that comes from the institutional church. You have the sense of people providing answers to questions that no one has asked and not hearing the questions that people are asking.

The same thing would be true of the statements of the American hierarchy. I don't mean the letters on peace or the economy, but the routine statements that come from them. They're written in a very opaque style.

There's not much reflection—to refer to one of my major themes—there's not enough reflection on the presence of grace in secular life. It is as though grace only happens in the church, that God only discloses himself—His Spirit only dances—in the church. Theologically, that's not true, but unfortunately that's the implicit model and the implicit perspective in most ecclesiastical statements.

What stylistic changes would you suggest?

You've got to do these things so that the 600 to 650 word press association dispatch and the 30 to 90 second television clip can say it all. That critical point occurs to none of them. Make it big, make it long, footnote a lot, quote yourself—then you've got an important document—that seems to be their perspective.

It isn't going to play in Peoria. They've no sense, I'm afraid, of the importance of the media in carrying their message. According to a study of American Catholics done by the *National Catholic Reporter* before the Pope came, only 30 percent of those polled had heard of the two pastoral letters on nuclear weapons and poverty. That's real failure. Part of the reason is the complexity of the documents.

You did say somewhere, though, that the bishops' peace pastoral did have a positive impact on Catholic attitudes.

There was a shift in Catholic attitudes in favor of peace in the wake of the pastoral. The before-and-after measures for the year that the peace pastoral was issued showed a considerable increase in the number of Catholics that thought too much money was being spent on nuclear weapons. Opposition went up nine or ten percentage points.

But that's not at all inconsistent with saying that only 30 percent of Catholics have even heard about it. You can indeed be influenced by what the bishops said without having read or even being very conscious of a particular pastoral letter.

Whatever effect those pastorals had, it was an effect that was mediated through television, the newspapers and news magazines. That's sort of a basic phenomenon of modern communication which I don't think the hierarchy realizes. They get to their people, not through the pulpit on Sunday, but through the news clip and news story and the column in *Time* or *Newsweek*.

What about the issue of dissent in the church? The Pope raised it on his trip when he indicated that—I can't quote exactly—that Catholics cannot dissent from papal teachings.

But they do. As we used to say in the mother tongue, *Ab esse ad posse valet illatio.* That means "From the fact, one argues to the possibility." People do dissent; therefore it's possible to dissent.

If you dissent, do you stop being a Catholic?

Of course not. The only way you can stop being a Catholic according to church law is to renounce your faith formally and join another. Nobody is doing that. So they don't stop being Catholic. Do you stop being a good Catholic? What's a good Catholic? Who judges that? Presumably God judges it.

You can ask if folks stop being obedient Catholics when they dissent, and I would say yes, that's true. The laity who do dissent in their marital lives and on the birth control teachings can no longer fairly be called obedient Catholics.

Would you change the way we elect the Pope?

Yes. I'm not sure how I would change it, though. In the tenth century they had a wonderful way of doing it. The parish priests of Rome would assemble in Saint Peter's and choose one in their number, usually, to be the new bishop.

Then they would bring him out on the balcony, not to be cheered enthusiastically by crowds as now happens, but to have their choice ratified by the people. If the crowds cheered, they went in and enthroned him. If the crowds booed, they went back and chose someone else.

So the people of Rome demanded and received, for a long, long time, the right to ratify the choice.

How did we get to the super-secret process we have now?

The present secret, sealed-up nature of the conclave only dates to the turn of this century. It was caused by the fact that the representative of the Austrian Empire entered the conclave and exercised the imperial veto of somebody who might have been elected Pope.

We don't have an Austrian emperor anymore, so it's time for a change.

How would you change it?

There ought to be a much broader electoral base. You can go two ways. You can say he's the Bishop of Rome and therefore the parish priests and the people of Rome ought to elect him. Or you can say that he's de facto become the Bishop of the world. In that case, the laity and the clergy of the world would have some right to participate.

Saint Leo issued a dictum of church law which says, "He who presides over all should be elected by all." Any violation of that was sinful.

The present form, in which most of us are not consulted, may be great theater—white smoke, black smoke, all of those things—but it's not, following Saint Leo, a moral way to elect the Pope.

Switching to bishops, this is what Andrew Greeley once had to say about bishops: "With a few notable exceptions, the hierarchical leadership exists as a spectrum running from mediocre to psychopathic."

That's a rather modest and moderate statement! But isn't that self-evidently true? Doesn't anybody who has to deal with bishops know that's true?

How does it happen that we get bishops like that?

How does it happen that universities get incompetent presidents, departments get poor to psychopathic chairman? It's part of the human condition. We're not very good at selecting leaders. It's aggravated by the fact that what Rome wants now is not good bishops, but safe bishops. Bishops that "no rocka the boat," with all due respect for Italians.

I take it from having read your writings that bishops tend to be more conservative than their priests?

But that's not surprising, of course, because bishops are selected precisely because they're conservative.

Rome's choice of bishops is obsessed now with two things—their attitude towards birth control and towards the ordination of women, which, you all know, is the essence of Catholicism! Since most priests see nothing wrong with birth control and think women ought to be ordained, you are going to have bishops who are either notably to the right of their priests, or bishops who have been able to see the Vatican about their positions.

Of the bishops of Chicago that you knew, the one you admired most was Stritch or Meyer?

Meyer. He was a scholar, a gentleman and a brave man. Sane.

What about his administrative ability?

He was a very, very effective administrator. He wasn't here very long and he had to spend a lot in Rome during the council, but he seemed to be able to choose good men, gifted people, and to give them the freedom they needed to do the job. So he was darn near the perfect bishop.

If he had lived, both the archdiocese and the American church would be very different. He died in 1965 at the age of sixty-one, so he had fourteen years ahead of him. He would have been archbishop of Chicago up until about 1980. That might mean, in effect, Meyer retiring and presumably being replaced by Bernardin—it would have been a very, very different church.

Putting aside for a minute your personal relationship with Cardinal Bernardin, how do you think he's been for the archdiocese of Chicago?

There's no cruelty in Joe Bernardin. There's no meanness and there's no authoritarianism. Nobody is hurt deliberately. In fact, if someone is hurt at all, it's their own fault. It's awfully hard to dislike Joe.

I probably have more reason than most for disliking him, but I still have to work at it. I doubt very much he will give a direct order ever. If he should give a direct order on occasion, it's always something that you can stand up and argue with him about. In that respect, he's a very gentle and democratic leader. After twenty years of craziness and cruelty under Cody, that's an enormous blessing.

What are the minuses?

Unfortunately, he does not seem to be able to stir up any sense of direction among priests. You get no feeling that he has any vision, certainly no vision that inspires you. Part of that is that he does not deal directly with the worst kinds of problems. The vocation shortage. The financial problem. The pedophile priest problem.

He has surrounded himself with people who wouldn't do a mean thing in the world, but who are not competent, qualified or certified for their work. So it tends to be a free, inept bureaucracy. A lot of papers get shuffled, but not much gets done. Nothing touches on the big problems of the church, even the big administrative problems.

So, what's your advice to the Cardinal?

He hasn't asked me for advice and is not likely to do so. If there were a serious request for advice, it might take a manuscript as long as this book is going to be. The most important one is that he should stop being afraid of talented people.

The thing about mediocre people is they don't offend others. Joe doesn't want to offend anybody. If he searched for talented people to advise him, their very presence would offend a fair number of priests in the diocese, and Joe doesn't want to run that risk. That's a terrible mistake.

I know for a fact that you and he were close personal friends way back, at least ten or fifteen years ago. Do you want to talk about why you think that friendship broke down after he became cardinal of Chicago?

Were we? Were we friends, you think?

When I saw you two in operation, it certainly seemed that way.

I will confess that I thought so too. But now I'm not so sure. I'm not sure that you can be a close friend with an archbishop.

Now, I chose those words, "I'm not sure," carefully. I don't know anymore because the way he has treated me since he came to the diocese makes me wonder if friendship can possibly mean to him the same thing it would mean to you and me.

That's interesting because I'm sure I even heard the words come out of his mouth that he was your friend.

Yes, I've heard him say it, and others have heard him say it. He doesn't act like one.

Something happened?

Yes. He came to Chicago. Before then, he said, "The trouble with the things Andy says, the criticisms he makes, is that they're usually true."

Now he tells people that the only problem is the novels.

That's surprising to hear.

If he still considers himself a friend, I could only say that he's a very timid friend, and he doesn't stand by you when you're being criticized and under attack. When the lights go out in the barroom, you know, that tells you who the friends are and who aren't.

Explain that?

When the lights go out in the barroom?

I've never heard the expression.

It's probably Irish. Lots of people can go around pretending they're friends. But it's only when the lights go out in the barroom and they start throwing the chairs and the knives, then you can tell who your friends are and who are not your friends.

XVI

PRIESTS

"They're battered, they're hurting, they don't have much hope for the future, and they're not terribly interested in recruiting young men to follow them."

Andrew M. Greeley when he was ordained.

What's happening to the priesthood of today?

It's in terrible disarray. The morale of the priests is awfully, awfully low. They're battered, they're hurting, they don't have much hope for the future, and they're not terribly interested in recruiting young men to follow them. While that's not true of everybody, it's a fair characterization of the average—very, very low morale.

The euphoria of the Vatican Council was blighted in this emphasis on the role of the laity in the church. A lot of priests don't see any particular special thing for them to contribute.

The younger priests, who have gone through the seminary in the post-Vatican II era, and, I presume, have the theological answers, often get very, very disheartened because they look around at the structure and the culture of the priesthood and say, "Hey, I don't want to be part of this."

Clerical culture is permeated by envy. It emphasizes mediocrity; it sanctions anyone who is mediocre. Right now, it's not a very appealing culture at all. So, the situation is bad.

Are those the reasons why there are so many people leaving the priesthood?

It's why some of them left, and why some still leave—discouragement. It is, even perhaps more to the point and more serious, the reason why priests aren't recruiting other young men to be priests.

The recruitment by priests of other young men—is that the principal source of vocations to the priesthood?

Priests and mothers. Most priests, and most young men who are thinking of being priests, will cite these as the two influential sources of their vocation: their mother and their parish priest.

Does that vary with ethnic groups?

There may have been different rates, but certainly, in each of the ethnic groups, those were the most two important figures. There was no ethnic group where you could say the parish priest doesn't matter, or mother doesn't matter. They both mattered. They both mattered in all groups more than anybody else.

I was wondering about the Italian-Americans?

The Italian-American mother is pretty powerful.

Oh, she sure is, but I didn't know she was encouraging her son to become a priest.

Oh, but if she does, the odds go up that he will become one. That's the point.

If you wish to improve the level of satisfaction with the parishes in the archdiocese of Chicago, would you do it by improving the counseling skills of the clergy?

The two big things people expect from priests are counseling—I don't mean sexual or therapeutic counselling, I mean sensitive and sympathetic understanding—and preaching.

Preaching is by far the more serious problem. My dissatisfaction with the quality of preaching is enormous. I said to Cardinal Bernardin, the one time I talked to him, "You've got to do something about preaching."

And he said, "What would you do?"

I said, "That's an unfair question which I refuse to answer because I don't know the answer."

Preaching is an exercise of the creative intuition. All of us are born with creativity, but with priests, their seminary training, their work and clerical culture have virtually destroyed their creativity. It's very, very difficult for a priest to sit down and write creatively. He's never learned how and his natural abilities to do so have never been amplified.

Doesn't your data show that one of the most important activities of the priest is preaching?

Yes. It has a stronger effect on people's religious behavior than any other factor. It doesn't matter what the Pope and Vatican say. The two strongest correlates of religious behavior are local. One is the behavior of the spouse, and the other is the quality of the local preacher. Absolutely essential.

What about celibacy? Is that a stumbling block for young men who want to become priests?

It surely is. What I question is whether it's any more a stumbling block now than it was fifty years ago.

Sex was not discovered in 1965. Young men born after the end of the Second World War, born after 1945, weren't the first young Catholics in America to discover that women were attractive. Celibacy has always been a problem for vocational recruiting. I don't think it's any more of a problem now than ever.

What about married priests?

Sure, if you could have married priests, we would have them coming out of our ears. We would have more priests than we know what to do with, as do most of the Protestant denominations—all of them.

If you're a Lutheran, you have to wait years and years and years to even get an associate's or co-pastor's assignment in a parish. As the kids would say these days, there are tons of vocations! We would have them too.

We would have had twice, three times, four times as many priests fifty years ago, twenty-five years ago, if we didn't have celibacy.

So, I don't see the problem today as the result of clerical celibacy. The problem today is the result of discouraged priests, alienated mothers, and the absence of dedicated and committed recruitment.

Will the church ever permit a married priesthood?

Do you know the joke about one cardinal asking the other that, and the response was, "No, but our children will live to see it"?

What I would like to see is this question settled at the national level rather than internationally. I'm sure if it were settled at a national level there would be some countries where there would be celibate clergy, and others where there would not.

We've already discussed your proposition about the short-term for Pope and bishop. Would that—

That'd solve the shortage.

How would it work?

A limited-term service would be a "Priest Corps" like the Peace Corps: "Come be a priest with us for five years, volunteer for five years." The evidence shows that if we did that, we would have enough priests. But there's not a chance in the world of that happening now.

Would they remain priests?

Yes, you'd be a priest forever, but you'd not be bound to exercise that ministry all the time. So, you'd be a priest, and maybe they could still call on you to hear confessions at Eastertime—which I guess isn't a necessity anymore—or in cases of emergency. But you wouldn't, after your term of office was up, have to exercise the priesthood, save on occasion.

' *Does the priesthood attract a certain type of person?*

It attracts altruists—people whose original orientations are generous. I don't think there's much doubt about that. But then, after they're ordained, they are not required to meet professional performance standards, the kind that are taken for granted in other professions.

I'm not going to say that all doctors, lawyers, dentists, military officers or professors are models of professional virtue. But there are standards of performance which would not tolerate the kind of mediocrity that is often taken for granted among priests.

The American Bar Association, the American Medical Association, for example, the American College of Surgeons—they have professional standards about which they're reasonably serious. We don't. Priests don't get sanctioned for lousy preaching.

Who do you think the board of review should be for priests?

Most importantly, their own parishioners. There should be real reviews, with teeth in them; the laity should have a major part to play in such reviews.

What are some reasons for staying in the priesthood?

The last ditch reason for staying in is not to give your enemies the satisfaction of leaving!

But that's not why I stay. I stay because I like being a priest. I've always liked it, and I still like it.

The other reason is that you've made a commitment. And even in the bad times, commitments are to be honored. I'm appalled at how easily in contemporary America people disregard commitments to wives, to children, to parents, or to the priesthood. I won't judge any individual case, but it does seem to me that a lot of men have left the ministry without much agony over violating a commitment. On the other hand, oftentimes, for someone to leave the active ministry is a wise decision, a mature decision, but still a violation of commitment.

Priests and politics?

John Carroll, the first bishop, said that on the whole he thought priests ought to stay out of politics because he didn't think they had the kinds of skills that were required to be good politicians. I would agree with that though I'd note that after he said that Bishop Carroll then went as an ambassador from the Continental Congress to the Canadians, with Ben Franklin and someone else. So he was certainly capable of some kind of involvement despite those principles.

I feel—and this is a matter of personal taste I suppose—that in our society the Catholic priest is advised to practice restraint in politics. He ought to stay out of it, save in very rare circumstances. I believe priests ought to be very, very cautious about political involvement.

Why?

When priests become involved as candidates, for issues or for parties, then there is a suggestion that the church, the gospel or the Lord God are on the same side. I don't think that's true. God likes Democrats more than Republicans, but She's tolerated both! She, personally, is a Democrat.

That's a relief to know. What about bishops in politics? I'm not necessarily thinking of individual bishops, but bishops as a group?

A fortiori, what I said would apply to bishops. They should stay the hell out of politics except in very, very rare circumstances. Even on the matter of abortion, where the church's convictions are pretty powerful, I'm not sure bishops should get involved in supporting or opposing specific kinds of anti-abortion legislation.

The ordinary priest—does he lead the same kind of life as the priests in your novels?

Blackie Ryan, my priest detective, chorus, herald, works pretty hard as a priest. We know he preaches, and he does all the good things a good pastor does, but still he's different. He is a confidante of the cardinal; he is a detective; he knows everybody that's anybody in Chicago; he comes from a wild and crazy but very close family. So, no, Blackie is not a typical priest.

What Blackie and his priesthood represents is the priesthood at it's best. It's intelligence, it's maturity, it's generosity, it's wisdom. One of the scholars who examined my novels said, "Blackie is Everyman." Rather, Blackie is more Everypriest. Not in the sense of being the typical priest, but in having some of those characteristics which the priesthood manifests at its best.

What kind of social interaction do priests have with women?

There was a time when I would not, even in Roman collar, have lunch with a woman. I may have been a little stricter then, but that would have been true with lots of priests. Now I have no problem about going to the opera or to the symphony with a woman. I'm not bothered in the least. I'd still wear the Roman collar, but lots of people wouldn't do that.

I suppose some have mistresses—probably lower rates of that than existed most times and most places in Catholic history.

Some have very, very close women friends, which, at least in some instances, seems to work pretty well. Still others, I suspect, really don't have any meaningful relationships at all. They don't trust women, or they don't like them, or they're afraid of them, or they resent them. They are kind of chauvinist bachelors. But I would be hesitant to put any numbers on that paradigm.

What about the social interaction of the priest with other men who are not priests?

In my generation, the principal role opposites of priests are either other priests or ex-priests from their class.

It may be the case, in younger generations, that they have more friends who are not priests. It's my impression, however, that most priests still choose most of their close friends from the presbyterate.

What about those who leave the priesthood? Did you do any studies on that?

Yes, we did some of that. It was in the 1969-70 study, so it's been a while. We could not find many differences in their level of marital satisfaction than those enjoyed by married laymen who had been married for the same number of years and entered marriages at about the same age as the priest did. They were neither happier nor less happy than the roughly comparable lay groups.

I don't know if your data tell you this, but were they happy with their decision to leave the priesthood?

They seem to be, yes. One of the sets of questions we asked is about their willingness to exercise the ministry again. If you could be a married priest, would you come back to the priesthood? More than half would say no, and only 20 percent said they would want to do the same things they had been doing as priests.

The image we often get is of the man, who, if he could still be a priest and marry, would go back to doing the things he was doing. My point is that this is a distinct and relatively small minority. Most of those who left the priesthood were not happy in the priesthood, and they don't want to go back to doing things that made them unhappy. It was not marriage, in great part, that caused them to leave; it was unhappiness that made them want to marry and then to leave.

In these people who have left the priesthood, have there been any changes in attitudes towards moral behavior, towards issues that they held when they were priests?

It's my impression that most of them are very devout, dedicated Catholics. They go to church, they send their kids to Catholic schools, they might be active members of their parish. And they may be, in some respects, more conservative than those of us who are still in the priesthood.

XVII
POLITICS

"Your image of God affects how you vote."

Mural

Andrew M. Greeley

If I'm correct, there is hardly any mention of politics at all in your autobiography, Confessions of a Parish Priest.

I do say that during the late sixties and early seventies I felt totally out of it because the politics of the younger generation, the politics of the sixties people, the politics of church folk—they were all the politics of the Berrigans—were confrontation and demonstration, rather than building coalitions.

Is coalition building a peculiarly Catholic style of politics?

Chicago ethnic that I am, I've been raised believing in coalition building. That was and is the Catholic political style. But like a lot of other things Catholic, we abandoned that eighteen or twenty years ago in favor of moralism, class conflict and a lot of other things which are foreign to our tradition.

Are you a political animal?

I'm interested in politics. I have friends who are politicians. But I don't know that I'm a particular political animal. I don't know that I'd be very good in the political process.

People keep asking, "When are you going to write your novel about Chicago politics?"

I say, "Never," because I don't know enough about it from the inside.

The people in my novels tend to be on the fringes of politics. There are political lawyers, for example. Priests like Blackie Ryan know politicians, but they don't run for office. They don't run cities. They don't sit on committees in Washington.

Yet you've been a serious commentator on politics in your columns. You've shaped a lot of political attitudes through them.

I don't think I shaped any attitudes from the columns. I'd be surprised at that. What kinds of political things have I commented about?

I don't have your columns in front of me, but I remember that you did columns on Carter and the Catholics, for example.

One of my hats is that of social commentator.

Jimmy Carter never did understand Catholics and never did realize how important Catholics were to his coalition. In that respect he was like most Democratic liberals of the era who would welcome Jews and blacks, gays, lesbians, but not Catholics. Yet, in terms of raw numbers, Catholics are the largest component of the Democratic coalition.

That's the kind of social commentary that I would make.

Did you endorse any candidates?

You won't find me either endorsing candidates or taking stands on specific political issues.

I'll take stands on immigration, for example, because the Simpson-Mazzoli bill was a disgrace. People that got here first excluding others! That's a terrible violation of the American spirit. But by and large, I don't endorse candidates or take stands on particular legislation. I don't feel qualified to do so and that generally, priests should stay out of that.

You do make policy suggestions, though.

There are certain policy issues on which I have an opinion, but they are generally not opinions that could be identified with one party or the other.

I've been saying for years what is increasingly being said now, that the United States will never balance its budget as long as it feels constrained to defend not only itself, but also the Europeans. Twenty years ago, I thought that made a hell of a lot of sense and I still do.

Eisenhower, Patton, Bradley—the whole leadership of our triumph in Europe during the World War II would be utterly astonished to be told that four decades later we would still have the 7th Army in Europe.

You're a Democrat, aren't you?

Yes, indeed. I don't pretend not to be a Democrat. I've never voted for a Republican candidate and probably never will.

Would you endorse someone like Mario Cuomo?

It's a big temptation.

I have to give him great credit because he's accomplishing two things. First, he is saying the truth, that you cannot run for office and be governor of New York. So he's assaulting this whole crazy two-year primary system. Second, he's also, it turns out, engaging in a remarkably shrewd political strategy, because everybody is waiting for Mario to drop the other shoe.

I also think our former governor from Arizona, Bruce Babbitt, would make a fine President.

Do you think Cuomo has a chance of being nominated?

All the other guys—the seven dwarfs—look so bad. After seeing the clips from the TV debate, I conclude that none of those guys could be nominated. It's either going to be Mario, Bill Bradley or, arguably, Sam Nunn. Nunn would be less popular than Bradley or Cuomo because he is a Southern conservative. But at least he would probably do much better than these seven dwarfs. It's not fair to Babbitt, I guess to link him with the other nerds. Six dwarfs.

Do you think there is any political possibility of that happening at this late date?

If any one of them has time to enter the New York, California, New Jersey and possibly even the Illinois primaries, and overwhelmingly carry those states, then it would be awful hard to deny him the nomination.

What do you think of Michael Dukakis?

Well, he just might be a Greek Mario Cuomo.

They're talking about the Super Tuesday as being extremely decisive.

But Super Tuesday is South! I don't think that's going to shape things all that much. Jesse Jackson will probably get the most votes and then all the others will be split.

If none of those noncandidates make it, what then?

How does one choose? Of the lot, I prefer Bruce Babbitt of Arizona because I know him and because he does speak the truth. He's not very smooth and he has a hard time with his television presence. He doesn't have all that much money. But he seems to me to be the most realistic of the lot.

I was very impressed by what I read about his political philosophy in The Washington Post.

Yeah, he's one of us. Class president from Notre Dame.

Let's get back to Mario. What do you think about him capturing the imagination of America?

He has wit and intelligence. He's clearly a very bright man. He's compassionate. He has re-articulated the old New Deal vision in a manner which suggests financial responsibility. And his notion of family, which is the theme that shaped his New York campaigns, is very appealing.

Family seems to be a central symbol in his political philosophy.

He's calling for a political order which emphasizes trust and a sense of responsibility.

What about Mario's roots?

You tell me about them! He's an Italian-American, Catholic, Thomist mystic from Queens.

I hadn't thought of him in terms of being a mystic.

The most moving section in his political diaries is where he describes his terrible discouragement when his father died during a campaign.

He went up to his father's room and finds his father's business card. His father owned a store. He didn't need business cards, but he had one.

Then he thinks of the time they moved into the new house. Lightning struck one of the blue spruces in the yard, and it fell down in the street. Then, in marvelous detail, he describes how he, his father and his brother pulled the tree back up, sank it back into the ground, staked it down, and kept it erect. There it still is, sixty-five feet high.

Then he says he put the card away and could hardly wait to get back into the campaign. That's symbolism. That's mysticism. Beautifully done.

Do his roots have anything to do with his political philosophy?

Sure.

What about one of your other political heroes, Mayor Richard Daley?

The mayor?

The *mayor. What was it about him that you admired?*

I thought he was the best municipal administrator in his generation of Americans. Like all human beings, he had faults and he made mistakes. But he combined two qualities that are rarely found in combination these days: marvelous administrative abilities and real political skills.

Why did he have so many enemies?

Not in Chicago. He was re-elected by overwhelming majorities. His enemies outside the city objected to the fact that he was Irish, Catholic and neighborhood-oriented. All of those things offend the kinds of deracinated liberals who tend to pontificate in the mass media.

Despite them and despite their bigotry, he won every election with between 65 and 75 percent of the votes. He carried the black and white wards overwhelmingly. He carried Jewish wards against Jewish candidates. He was enormously popular in the city.

Irish-Catholic politicians are a kind of standard ink blot for American liberals, as is the city of Chicago. That includes the liberal carpetbaggers that come from other parts of the country to live and work here, and to operate our institutions and corporations. It also includes the self-hating alienates who grew up in Chicago, went to universities and are ashamed to be from Chicago. As you can see, I am none of the above!

Would you describe the Daley machine?

The mayor of Chicago does not have much statutory power. We have a weak-mayor, strong-council form of government. The mayor's capability in getting things done depends entirely on the personal power he is able to amass. Daley amassed enormous personal power which he used to get things done, mostly by being a master of tradeoffs— I'll do you a favor, you do me a favor. I'm obligated to you, you're obligated to me.

What about the precinct system?

The precinct and the ward committeemen are a network of modules where tradeoffs can occur. So if you need the street fixed, you call the precinct captain or the ward committeeman to get it fixed. It's a sort of a decentralized, informal government which makes the bureaucracy function.

In a way, the senator and the representative play the same role in Washington. If some federal agency isn't treating you properly—in other words, isn't giving you that to which you have the right—then you call your congressman or you write your senator and they make inquiries. They have people on their staffs whose whole job is to deal with the complaints that come from their constituents.

Is the system still operating in Chicago?

It's hard to tell because of the peculiar nature of our politics for the last few years. It still works in some neighborhoods.

The Chicago style of politics—is it peculiar to Chicago?

It would be peculiar to any big city in the Northeast and the central part of the country where you have lots of ethnic diversity and relatively small electoral districts.

Is municipal politics different in Tucson?

Yes, because there's no network of communities at all comparable to what we have.

It's very heavily media politics without that much grassroots organization. So far. The city keeps growing. There are always new people there. The power bases simply haven't emerged yet.

What's the appeal of the Democratic party to Catholics?

It is the party that recruited them when they came in, the party that was willing to accept them. The Republican party was essentially the WASP party and the Democrats became the Catholic party.

It's still the Catholic party?

Yes, the majority of Catholics are Democrats. The majority of Catholics routinely vote Democratic.

Is there a change among the young Catholics in their political affiliation? Are they becoming more independent?

They're more likely to identify as independents, but as you look at their voting patterns in congressional and senatorial elections, they still, by and large, vote Democratic.

Do they eventually affiliate themselves with the Democratic party?

There are not very many dues-paying party members for either party. There are not many card-carrying Democrats because there are no cards to carry.

An identification is merely the way you answer a survey question. It is fashionable to say you're independent. That way you seem to be somebody that's intelligent and keeping your options open. But I see no particular changes in the proportion of young Catholics who routinely vote Democratic, however they describe their affiliation.

Has there been any kind of decline in Democratic alignment?

What may have declined is the "Yellow Dog Democrat," or, as I call them here in Chicago, the "Junk Yard Dog" Democrats. A "Junk Yard Dog" Democrat is somebody who would vote for a junk yard dog so long as he was on the Democratic ticket.

I'm being partly facetious when I say that, but I'm also being partly serious because party affiliation is an important prop of political life. The country suffers when party affiliation declines.

Will you talk about national politics and Ronald Reagan?

I don't have much to say on the subject, but I'll be happy to talk.

How did he become President?

He became President, first of all, because he was running against Jimmy Carter, which was an easy thing to do. And because he was running against inflation, which was outrageously high, mostly because Carter had bungled the economy, and he was running against the Ayatollah Khomeini, who had Carter over a barrel. Again, most of that was Carter's fault.

As Eisenhower won his first election because he was running against Truman and the Korean War, so Reagan got elected the first time because he was running against Carter, Iran and inflation.

What about Reagan's reelection?

He might have been beatable in the second election, but certainly not by Walter Mondale. The Democrats came up with a very weak candidate there.

Moreover, he was a popular President by that time. Inflation virtually vanished. The Ayatollah wasn't—it seemed then—hassling us anymore. Reagan was and is a charming, gregarious man. Taxes were being cut. All kinds of good things were happening. So he was viewed as a successful and popular president. He was reelected against a very weak opponent—the kind of candidate the Democrats seem destined to offer every four years.

Does he show an ethnic style in this Presidency?

I have to be careful of that because he is, after all, Irish! There's something about that smile and charm of his that suggests Irish. But it's more a movie-actor style.

What about the Reagan revolution? Has there been one?

Not that I can see. One keeps reading about America turning to the right or the conservative counter- revolution. As a survey-taker and a data-reader, I see no evidence of this.

American attitudes may have become more conservative on two issues: gun control and the death penalty. We've moved from having a majority opposed to the death penalty to now having four-fifths in favor of it.

These are both crime-related issues. They are a protest against crime in the streets and in the city, something about which people are very concerned.

Is that all?

I can't imagine other issues on which Americans have become conservative. Sexual practices have become more cautious and conservative. But that's not because of the Reagan revolution. That's because of AIDS and herpes. So all of this hoopla about Americans being more conservative—the rise of the Moral Majority, the turn to the right—all these things are media constructs which have little to do with reality.

Has Reagan turned back the New Deal?

I don't know in what respect it could be said that he did. Certainly, he has—and most Americans would welcome it—tried to put a limit to the expansion of the federal government. Big government doesn't have quite as much easy access to money as it did. A lot of that has finally come to no effect because he's put so much more money in the Pentagon sinkhole.

But the things the New Deal stood for—social security, etcetera—they're still in place.

What about the Reagan legacy?

The next President, whoever he is, is going to have to engage in some reordering of priorities. We simply cannot be a world empire. Nobody can play that game anymore. In various parts of the world we're going to have to cut down on military spending. We're going to have to reallocate funds to some areas of civilian life that the Reagan years have neglected.

In 1976, when nobody knew which way the Catholic vote was going to go because we had, for the first time, an evangelical Baptist candidate for President, you predicted exactly how the Catholic vote would go.

How did you do that? Are you aware that you predicted it exactly?

No, I'm not. I'm glad I did. If I did it was simply because I had looked at past results and projected them into the present. I figured Carter would win, but barely.

In 1984, you claimed you got final proof of religion being a good predictor of behavior in many areas, including politics.

That was a result of the work that I did on religious imagination indicators which I inserted in the National Opinion Research Center's General Social Survey.

How you picture God has a very significant effect on your attitudes towards capital punishment, racial justice, civil liberties, and also, how you vote in elections. If you picture God as a mother or lover, you would be 15 percentage points more likely to vote for the Ferraro/Mondale ticket.

That's true whether you were a Democrat or Republican, or whether you describe yourself as a liberal or conservative. Obviously, if you're a conservative Republican, you're not very likely to vote for Ferraro and Mondale. But if you have an image of God as a lover and a mother, you would be more likely to vote for them than Republican conservatives who do not picture God as a lover and a mother.

You can run that through every combination of liberal, conservative, Democrat, Republican and come up with the same findings—that your image of God affects how you vote.

That's incredible.

I liked it.

That was picked up by Gallup, wasn't it?

He used it in the—was it the 1984 election?—and got roughly the same findings, but he hasn't done anything with it since. Other survey analysts are beginning to use it. Articles are beginning to emerge.

I'd like to ask some religious questions about politics. Is Jesus' message relevant to politics or to political action?

He certainly hasn't given us a stand to take on the trade bill. Jesus is not going to be able to tell us next week when Mr. General Secretary Gorbachev comes, what kinds of verification requirements are adequate and what aren't adequate. What I'm saying here is that I don't think you can derive from the gospel stands on specific issues. I don't think that can be done.

Religion is relevant to politics in terms of orientations and commitments. Religion in that way certainly makes a contribution to political involvement and political style. But it rarely gives you answers on specific issues.

Sure you have to be against racial segregation. You have to be against nuclear war. But how best to avoid nuclear war? I don't think there are any answers to that. Men and women of good will and good faith can disagree.

What do you think about the political ramifications of the abortion issue?

There's a consensus here in the country now for some legislation which would limit it, say, to the first three months. From the point of view of Catholics, that might be a very unsatisfactory compromise. But if it's attainable, I don't think it's up to bishops to say aye or nay because what do they know about what's attainable? If it's that or nothing, that ought to be a decision that's left to the wisdom of individual citizens and individual legislators to determine for themselves.

What do you think about the kinds of actions the bishops in the Philippines took with Marcos?

I'm not a Filipino. I'm certainly sympathetic with what they did. It's a whole different situation. Early on in this part of our dialogue I talked about America, and that's the only country I would want to comment on.

Do you sense a loss of a sense of public commitment or concern, and an increasing focus on the private in American life?

No, this is the knock on us. You know that terrible book by Robert Bellah and his colleagues, *Habits of the Heart*—there's no empirical data to support their thesis at all. In fact, all the empirical evidence seems to me to go in the opposite direction.

But lots of clergy and theologians like to quote it as though it is an absolute authority, the way the Dominicans used to quote Saint Thomas. The thesis is demonstratively false. Americans are not more individualistic than they used to be.

214

What about the loss of sense of the public, though? A sense of obligation to public or a loss of the sense of common good? The stuff that the Senate was talking about?

I'm not convinced. I've never seen any data set that convinces me of that.

Have you seen data to demonstrate the opposite?

I look at civic and organizational participations. Those are all constantly going up in America. There are more neighborhood organizations and community organizations than every before. I'm inclined to think Americans are probably more involved in civic stuff than ever before.

My colleagues Sidney Verba and Norman Nie did a study about fifteen years ago on civic participation, which Bellah et al. cite, but apparently don't understand. Now Sidney and Norman are doing the same study again. This will give us time-series measures. We'll be able to see whether civic to political participation has increased or decreased. I'll give odds of twenty to one that it has not decreased and ten to one that it has increased. Such findings, alas, will not silence either Bellah or his clerical admirers.

Keeping that same study in mind, has there been a decline in the voting behavior of Americans?

It fluctuates. I suspect, though, that if you look at the age composition of the population—you have to because the population is disproportionately skewed because of the baby boom—if you take that into account, there hasn't been a decline. Younger people are less likely to vote than older people. So I don't think there's a change.

XVIII
CATHOLICISM

"Objects, events and persons are all relevatory of God; they are all metaphors for God. That's the Catholic sensibility."

Andrew M. Greeley at his sixtieth birthday party, February 1988.

You wrote a book, with your sister Mary G. Durkin, which you titled
How to Save the Catholic Church. *What's the answer to the question
you raised?*

We have to recapture our awareness of the Catholic religious sensibility, which is David Tracy's analogical imagination, if you wish. It
can pretty much be summarized in terms of the sacramentality of the
world. Objects, events and persons are all revelatory of God; they are
all metaphors for God. That's the Catholic sensibility. It differs from
the Protestant sensibility in that the Protestant sensibility emphasizes
the absence of God, the otherness of God, and we emphasize the
presence of God, the immanence of God, the incarnation of God.

Are these sharply contrasting sensibilities?

These are matters of emphasis, they're not matters of a sharp break.
But they are important matters.

Practically, what does it mean?

One way to indicate it is to point out that we have saints, we have
angels, we have a Blessed Mother, we have stained glass and statues.
We have all these things which Protestants, Jews and Islamic folk often
consider an abomination or idolatry.

What are the limits of these perspectives?

The other religious sensibilities feel that if you identify the holy,
the transcendent, with these creatures, then it will stop being transcendent. We respond that if you don't identify it with these creatures,
then the world becomes a bleak and empty place, which it truly does.

There are dangers in both sensibilities. The danger in ours is folk
religion and superstition. The miraculous medal becomes a worker of
miracles instead of a reminder. The saint becomes, not an image which
tells us the story of God, but someone to whom we offer gifts.

The danger in the other sensibility is the radical desacralization of
the world, the turning of the world into a bleak, empty and godless
place. Both emphases need each other, but they are still different emphases. We have to recover the Catholic position of sacramentality, re-
articulate it and celebrate it again.

*Where do you think that should happen? On what level in the
church?*

From the mother explaining the Christmas story to her kid on up to Pope John Paul II. Everywhere.

You've recently made some concrete suggestions about what should be done in liturgy, in an article in America *magazine.*

We should resurrect the angels, the saints, the souls in purgatory, the Blessed Mother and all of those wonderful stories of God's love.

The Blessed Mother represents the womanliness of God. The saints and the souls in purgatory represent the union among everybody in the human species—those who have already lived and those who are still alive.

The angels represent the existence of wonder and surprise. God sent them to care for each one of us. These are the kinds of things that are part and parcel of the Catholic tradition that most Catholics still like. Those things should be re-interpreted and re-articulated instead of being abandoned.

You make a suggestion about St. Valentine in that article.

We've really must rehabilitate him. He probably was a pagan love god at some point. Then we made him a Christian saint. Then the pagans took him back and he's now the patron of romantic love, which he's always been.

But he's a Catholic, a Catholic saint at that. We ought to reclaim him and make his day—which is the second busiest day of the year for restaurants—a day for the renewal of romantic love among our married people. We ought to have renewal of marriage vows and a Mass for husbands and wives and romantic parish dances on that day.

I had two of them in the article. One is to, at the beginning of the baptism ceremony, ask the parents to imagine the child can hear them. Have them tell the child how they feel about her birth and baptism and what they wish for her in life.

I have never seen that fail. It always elicits some of the most beautiful, tender, affectionate and edifying statements you could possibly imagine.

It is the role of the homilist or sacramental minister to respond to that, to re-collect it and to correlate it with the tradition.

Now it's being done on videotape. There you've got the parents' statement on baptism day to the kid, which she can play over and over and over again. It helps the child to know how they felt when he or she made their first appearance.

And the other suggestion?

I don't quite know how you do this logistically, but it struck me at the weddings I officiated at last year that the most moving and beautiful parts of the ceremony are the toasts at the banquet, where the bride toasts the groom and the groom toasts the bride. They are very, very lovely statements of affection.

I somehow think those should be transferred from the wedding banquet into the church. The role of the homilist would be the same, to re-collect these toasts and relate them to the tradition.

What changes would you like to see in the Sunday service?

I used to say a long time ago I'd like to see the pews pulled out of the church and tables and chairs put in so it really looked like a banquet. The Eucharist is, after all, a meal. It should be made to look like a meal.

We'd drop the three readings—one is more than enough for preaching. We'd drop the two psalms, because people don't know what they mean. We'd retire permanently all semiliterate readers, whether they be deacons or lay people. We'd only let people that can read read. We'd put the handshake of peace at the end of the Mass, or, perhaps better, at the beginning.

We'd hire good musicians so that we'd have good church music. They would be the kinds of musicians who believe in congregational singing and can teach congregations how to sing. We'd start commissioning people to write good music.

That all sounds good, but it also sounds like a lot more than people would put up with.

The genius of Roman liturgy is movement. Jungman, in his book on the origins of the Roman liturgy, made that point years ago. The Roman liturgy does not mess around. It moves. It has a style and a grace that comes from reasonably drafted rules. The Romans went in there, they did it and they were finished with it.

All dragginess, all moping, all long pauses, all slowing down the process of the movement of the Mass should be done away with. That's not for the sake of getting it done earlier and getting people out into the parking lots. It's that it is the genius of the Roman liturgy not to slow down and muck around. It does what is to be done and it's finished.

What do you think of liturgies that are in touch with the cultural nerve, like a black liturgy or a Polish liturgy? A Hungarian?

Fine. I have no problems with them. The same rules I've enunciated should apply to those, too.

In an earlier conversation, you pointed out that the church had, at one time, under certain circumstances, tolerated remarriage after divorce.

For example, when a man went off to war and didn't return. When somebody had an incurable disease. When a slave was freed.

So what would that suggest for contemporary attitudes to remarrying after divorce?

I don't know that it suggests anything specifically. It does simply show that those who say the church never tolerated marriage after divorce don't know any history.

Today, almost anybody that wants an annulment can get one. An ever-increasing number of priests are willing to grant their own annulments in the directory parlor in the name of the so-called "internal forum solution." So Catholics who now want to remarry after divorce and receive the sacraments can readily do so. That seems to be a satisfactory pastoral solution.

In theory, I guess the church should go back to where it was a thousand years ago and get the hell out of marriage legislation. That's a civil problem. It should be left to be decided civilly.

Individual cases of conscience should be left to the good judgment of parish priests, or maybe to the whole parish community. But the whole structure of ecclesiastical courts for annulments and separations is a medieval relic with which we could conveniently dispense.

Would you explain the "internal forum solution"?

It's a solution which has existed all along, but which we were urged in the seminary to use with caution.

You have a couple, one person of whom has been married before. They've tried, but for one reason or another, the ecclesiastical annulment process is not available to them. In good conscience and in good faith, after considering all the factors, the divorced person is convinced that that first marriage was not a sacrament and that therefore he or she would indeed be free to contract the valid sacrament.

The parish priest hears this in the internal forum—that means it's not a public decision, but it's not in the confessional either.

He thinks about it; they talk about it. He decides, "Yes, I agree with you that the first marriage was not a marriage and you are free to marry. Church law does not permit us to validate your marriage publicly, but nonetheless, you can renew your marriage vows and thus become husband and wife in the eyes of God, and receive the sacraments."

That's incredible! I had not heard about it.

It's been around all the time, and it's increasingly being used.

Has the church ever felt that human life did not begin from the first moment of conception?

I don't know what one means by the church here, because I don't think that is official Catholic teaching. I don't see how it can be official teaching because it's not a theological issue, it's a biological issue.

While the church is opposed to abortion, I believe the reason for the opposition is that we don't know when life begins, and since we don't, we have to make the assumption that it begins at the moment of conception. We have to make that assumption because there's the moral logical principle that you always have to err in the favor of life. But I don't know that it's even been Catholic doctrine that life begins at conception.

The theologians of the Middle Ages thought it took thirty days for a man and ninety days for a woman before the fetus was a human person. They thought that because of mistaken scientific assumptions. The present assumptions are based, as I see it, on the genetic notion that when you combine the sperm in the ovum, you have the program for a human person.

I don't know that it can be really insisted on as official Catholic teaching.

Why not?

The problem with it is, first of all, that there's so many spontaneous abortions; so many fertilized ova are lost through natural processes. That would suggest a lot of human souls are lost, if the egg were a human person from the moment of conception.

Then, secondly, we do know that up to a certain point in time, maybe two weeks after fertilization, a fertilized ovum can split and produce twins. Does that mean that this one human soul is split and becomes two human souls? That would present a lot of peculiar theological problems.

I say these things not to give any answers to the problem of abortion. I'm not a moral theologian; I don't feel myself confident to talk on those issues. But I do say that there is, on the basis of the human sciences, considerable reason to wonder whether the human person, that is to say the human soul, begins at the instant of conception.

You've said a few times in your writings that Catholicism means "Here comes everybody."

Yes.

What does that mean?

Where did I pick that up? Your man, James Joyce, has it someplace in one of his books.

It means that Catholicism—in its best moments, anyhow—defines the boundaries out as far as it can and welcomes every different kind of culture and language and custom that it can absorb. It is not a narrow and rigid and exclusive religion; it is a broad, permeable and inclusive religion.

Now, of course, it hasn't always practiced that. The French missionaries in China, who did such wonderful work for a couple of centuries, nonetheless felt that converting the Chinese to Catholicism also meant making them French. It came to the same thing, and even more so, in Vietnam where the Catholics were quasi-French.

We may have done the same thing—though perhaps less enthusiastically, less comprehensively and systematically than the French did—in our missionary work in the Orient. To become a Catholic meant to become a member of a parish that was not unlike one of your better Brooklyn or Boston or Chicago parishes.

We have not in recent centuries had as much respect for local cultures.

True or false: Catholics who become successful academically leave the church.

False. I've never been able to find any evidence of that. It may have been true earlier in the thirties and forties, but in all the research that we've done—four or five studies—in which we looked at college-educated Catholics and the Catholics that go on to academic careers, their defection from the church is no higher than anybody else's.

So, you've got all kinds of distinguished and eminent academics around the country now, people that are full professors, that seem to be approaching fifty even, who are practicing Catholics—members of their parish council, kids in Catholic schools.

The problem is the reverse: they don't leave the church, the church ignores them.

Why does the church ignore them?

We have produced, in the last quarter-century, a thriving Catholic intelligentsia of which the church leadership remains steadfastly unaware. They don't want to know about these intellectuals. Bishops who feel intellectually inferior, by and large, to anybody with an earned doctorate, and not without reason Heaven knows, have the living day-lights scared out of them by real intellectuals.

At the time you wrote your book, Crisis in the Church, *you said that if anybody read only one of your books, it should be this one.*

A lot of people didn't read it, but a lot of people haven't read any of my books. If they're priests or bishops, however, they know what's in them apparently without reading them!

What point did you make in the book?

It was a demographic, socioeconomic and religious portrait of Catholics, both nationally and locally, at the time that I wrote the book, eight or nine years ago.

It asked, What sort of Catholics do we have? Are they about to leave the church? The answer was no. Are they about to do what the church leaders tell them? The answer was no. What do they think of their clergy and that leadership? The answer was, not much. Are they still Catholic? The answer was, you bet!

Now, this model is finally beginning to be accepted. The surveys done at the time of the Pope's visit to this country richly confirmed that model. Some of the more literate bishops, not excluding my own, basically accept that to be true, although they would be afraid to admit it.

In that book, were you saying that there are different types of Catholics?

225

I can't remember precisely how I put it then, but what I would say now is that in a population of maybe sixty million Catholics, you have a wide variety of attitudes and beliefs, relationships to the church and relationships to God, running all the way from folks as conservative as Catholics United for the Faith to the *Commonweal* liberals and the liberation theologians.

It may not be possible for all of those people to make a legitimate claim to being Catholic, but they all do make the claim. Church leadership has to realize that there is this spectrum, and they also have to realize where most of the folks are in the spectrum.

I also think we have to restrain the efforts of some people to define Catholicism as being identical with their style and their style only. The attempt to do that sort of thing is certainly understandable—they'd want to get the massive weight of the Catholic tradition and community behind their particular set of beliefs—but it's not Catholic to be that exclusivist.

What do you think of the techniques of some of those Catholics to get their positions set up as the standard?

You mean the letter-writers?

Yes.

It's no secret that the leadership is intimidated to the point of paralysis by letters. They view their morning mail as an accurate description of the temper of the Catholic people. You really can't argue with them. I can say that as one who has tried.

You can tell them that only a certain kind of person writes letters, and they're usually the kind that don't like change. Most people don't write letters, and most of the people would not agree with the letter-writers.

Bishops worry about their mail a lot more than they should. They should worry about surveys, because surveys give you a random sample, mail doesn't.

Do you see a cycle in American Catholic life, a developmental cycle, young people tending to leave the church and then come back?

I don't think "leave" is the right word. They would still identify as Catholics, most of them. But there is certainly a life cycle, or an age-related cycle, in religious behavior.

That's the project Michael Hout and I are working on this year. The basic model we have shows religious behavior beginning to decline in the late teens. It reaches a low at about twenty-five, then begins to move up—indeed, rather sharply—until people are in their forties. Then, at about fifty, it levels off again, with maybe a slight decline in the older years as people get infirm.

That curve seems to be accurate thus far, fitting pretty all the variables we're looking at. Certainly, it fits church attendance and church affiliation.

How would you suggest the church relate to that pastorally?

In two ways. First of all, the church should be filled with good hope because the folks who drifted away are, by and large, going to come back. Almost nothing you can do to them is going to stop them from coming back.

Secondly, the church should prepare very carefully for their return. When people come back—to be married, or to have their kids baptized—it should be a glorious, celebratory event, instead of what it is now. Now, it is often a very awkward and painful event in which inept priests and inept nuns impose upon them rules and regulations and restrictions and guidelines that make return a difficult and unpleasant experience. I think that's horrendously insensitive.

You said the change apparently is age-related. It has nothing to do with marriage or children, or does it?

That's something that Mike and I aren't sure of. The work I've done previously suggests, as far as church attendance goes, marriage and children are not important. By the time you're thirty-five, whether you're married or not, or whether you have children or not, you're still likely to come back to church.

However, church affiliation—whether you identify as a Catholic or not—does indeed seem to be marriage-related. The reason why there's been an increase in the numbers of people who have no church affiliation in America is the declining marriage rates, the postponement of marriage, and the numbers of people who simply aren't married.

Is that a large number of people?

Let me give you a statistic about that. The group born in the fifties, the baby boomers, 20 percent of the women in that group are not yet married. Twenty percent! Twenty percent more are divorced and not remarried.

You have 40 percent of that population—women, basically in their thirties now—are not presently married, and they're not happy. That is, for me, a scary, scary statistic.

What's scary about it?

They're not happy.

How do you know that?

Because in our surveys they say that they are not happy. Being happy is strongly related to being married, according to the data. So you have a sixth of the population in general, and two-fifths of the population of that cohort who are acutely unhappy people—I should say, to be precise, who tend to be acutely unhappy—precisely because of the social changes which have depressed the marriage rate.

What should the church do about that?

I don't know. For those who have never married—I don't say this altogether facetiously—we should re-institute the novena in honor of St. Anne, which was a novena for unmarried women seeking a husband.

Maybe we've got to go back to running high clubs, and young adult clubs, bringing unmarried men and women together so that they can meet each other.

Most of the divorced women are likely to have children, and are likely to be acutely unhappy. They have been, for the most part, abandoned by their husbands. Or, in some cases, they have withdrawn from impossible relationships with their husbands. They are stuck with the children, and they are probably not getting the child support that they were guaranteed by the divorce settlement.

So, their husbands have gone off to a bachelor life or are remarrying, and these women are stuck with all kinds of problems. I don't know what the church can do to help them, but it sure as hell has got to figure out something to do.

Was there anything else you wanted to add about Catholicism, or Catholics?

I can sort of summarize. The Catholic community's heritage and tradition is in great shape. We have some good scholars, theologians, Scripture scholars.

But, the big problem is the lack of leadership, and that problem extends from the Vatican right on down to the parish, and most acutely in the parish . We not only need more priests, we need better priests: less cynical priests; more hopeful priests; more sensitive priests; more energetic priests; better preaching priests. There is no problem in the American church that's insoluble, if you have good priests.